to Paolo Villa

The Right *to* Nature

For a new urban landscape

Emanuele Bortolotti
Paolo Palmulli
with **Alessandro Frigerio**

Table of contents

Dwelling

Green welfare

Heritage

Care

Apparatus

Simona Galateo

AG&P greenscape, forty years of experience

Climate change is a problem that still shows evidence of its growing impact with each passing year. After believing for centuries that we could exploit the landscape with impunity, today, we have to deal with the consequences of this enormous error. Environmental degradation, growing social conflict, the loss of harmonious relations between human beings and nature, local identity, and the historical context have gradually emerged as essential themes to be tackled for a more liveable future. Adapting our cities and their infrastructure to these conditions of rapid environmental change is the principal challenge faced by the designers and planners of the 21st century.

What does it mean today, though, to design with nature under these conditions? Landscape architecture today, and this is going to be even more true soon, ought to serve as a guide to the overall development of the built environment, one that can promote a more systemic, historical, and evolutionary methodology and approach. The relations that humanity has with nature, the landscape and its cultural diversity, natural values, the conservation of the landscape heritage, the approaches and means required to plan for a more sustainable and integrated environment are key questions that have to be tackled by all the players involved in the processes of designing with Nature.

Taking up these challenges and responding to these problems following more than a decade of experience in the field, AG&P greenscape publishes the studio's seventh book, *The Right to Nature*. An opportunity to reflect on how to better address, with an integrated and multidisciplinary approach, the urgent issues of the environment that surrounds us and in which we live.

AG&P greenscape brings to its work an understanding of design that has evolved and matured over forty years of activity, with an approach that considers the concept of 'diffused landscape' as an operational tool, an interpretation of the contemporary city in which nature is an integrated and extended part of the available spaces in the entire built urban fabric.

Founded in Milan in 1985 as AG&P, *Architettura dei Giardini e del Paesaggio* (Garden and Landscape Architecture), by architect Paolo Villa and agronomist and garden designer Emanuele Bortolotti, the studio has tackled landscape design on every scale, from the garden to the city, to the region, taking on and handling all the different phases in the urban and environmental transformation of the contemporary city. The relationship between city and nature has changed as a result of the evolution in the form and dimensions of our urban fabrics. This resulted in the landscape adapting to changes in land use, with consequences that have often led to a gradual loss of the local identity.

Mainly located in Lombardy's capital city, the studio's first works were developed in years that were particularly interesting for Milan, which since the 1990s has been an urban laboratory of experimentation, an example among all other Italian and European cities in terms of innovation and transformation. Under these urban conditions, AG&P greenscape has acquired, in a competent and proficient way, the skills, tools and sensitivity that allow it to grasp and respond correctly to the complexities of landscape design. This resulted in a sartorial and artisanal approach constantly informed by research and theory, but also and above all by the practical aspects of construction.

Through meticulous planning of its interventions on different scales, the studio is a true experimental laboratory, which enables it to look at and deal with an ever more complex urban situation, developing an approach rooted in research, experimentation, and action, and in a continual dialogue and exchange of ideas with members of its own staff, the workforce, clients, and project partners.

Between the 1980s and '90s, unlike in many European countries, in Italy there was no real training course for landscape designers and much of the design of open spaces in the city had a distinctly architectural or urban-planning character. The figure of the landscape designer was not recognised professionally until 2001, when the country's Associations of Architects redefined the classes and categories of job titles in the profession, including landscape designers along with planners in an acknowledgement of the profound difference in expertise.

In this cultural milieu, the AG&P studio can be considered a pioneer in having taken a multidisciplinary approach to exploration of the landscape that drew on the fields of architecture and agronomy to find new spaces for design. In fact, the practice was among the first to establish a positive relationship with the private sphere, starting to create areas of natural environment of varying sizes in the urban fabric of Milan, a place for experimentation and research for more than twenty years. And in the same period, it laid the foundations for a first major project of landscaping, the Centroparco at Segrate, in collaboration with the public administration and a private investor: the realisation of a large urban park, a green lung, to preserve the existing natural environment and, with great foresight, reclaim a former quarry, as well as contain the pressure of local urban development.

With the arrival of the new millennium, the demands of work also changed for AG&P, in response to ever increasing numbers of commissions on an increasingly larger scale, taking up the challenge presented in those years by the urban scene in Milan, as well as in other parts of the country and abroad, that was undergoing rapid growth and transformation. When architect Paolo Palmulli joined the studio becoming general manager in 2008 and a partner in 2011, he started to organise the staff into different teams based on their skills and expertise to meet the requirements of each project.

In these years, and drawing upon work experiences that by now ranged between different scales of intervention, the concept of 'diffused landscape' took shape and was put into effect: an approach to design that reinforced the idea of a systemic nature, capable of creating synergies through all levels of the environment, from small gaps in the fabric to large areas, conceived as a precious and democratic resource that can re-establish a balance and host a new urban sociality. Bringing nature everywhere the soil and technology permit it, has become one of the studio's cultural missions.

With this vision, which is the outcome of many years of experience, AG&P increasingly expanded the scale of the projects it was working on. Commissions became more international, and the necessities of adapting to an ever-broader market led the studio, in 2016, to change its name to AG&P greenscape, highlighting an approach to landscape design that was increasingly focused on the presence of high quality and valuable greenery, systemically dispersed over the entire area.

The growing number of commissions, as well as their increasing scale, prompted the studio to take on the task of drawing up master plans for some of the most significant urban transformations in Italy. This led to it becoming an important point of reference in all the different stages of design: from the initial ones, including that of participation in competitions, to consultancy on the implementation of projects already underway, the supervision of works and assumption of responsibility for the maintenance and care of areas of landscaping.

Due to the increasing scale and degree of complexity required by urban and regional undertakings of regeneration and transformation, in 2022 the corporate and organisational structure of AG&P greenscape changed again. The organisational chart of the firm was altered to allow it to better respond to the different areas of expertise required by the work, and the architect and urban designer Alessandro Frigerio joined the management team, consolidating the studio's research capacities and experience and allowing it to move towards a programmatic and systemic vision of the landscape that would be increasingly attentive and sensitive to the urban and regional context.

Opening a new chapter in the firm's history also led to the need to publish a new book. *The Right to Nature* has been conceived as a manifesto which explores all the possibilities of the diffused landscape, a way of tackling the planning that is the fruit of forty years' experience in the field. The argument made in this work is not that the natural context has to be defended by treating the expansion of settlement solely as something that needs to be curbed. Instead, it aims to highlight the need for a more thorough and painstaking approach, one in which natural areas are also seen as a true driving force behind improvement in the quality of life in urban areas.

Intended as an all-round reflection on the methodological approach of the studio, the book is a concerted publication featuring various voices, which sets out to show how every intervention is the product of close collaboration between the practice, the project team, the client, the partners and all the workforce involved. The volume is introduced by an essay by landscape designer Gioia Gibelli, and texts in which three authors present some more general reflections about the book. These are followed by seven sections, turning around seven key concepts that sum up the categories of intervention in the landscape: 'Green and blue infrastructures', 'Regeneration', 'Public space', 'Dwelling', 'Green welfare', 'Heritage' and 'Care. Each chapter shows examples of the interventions carried out by the studio and is explored through a text introducing the theme, a key project, whose dynamics of development are described by the whole of the studio's team involved in the intervention, and by a number of parallel projects. Finally, a dialogue, with the client or a project partner. To close the volume, a text very dear to Paolo Villa, master of all things to do with trees and nature, who passed away in 2019.

Exploring the landscape through the different scales of its design helps us to understand the true complexity and holistic nature of the system we call the Earth and to recognise the impact humanity has on it. Only in this way will it be possible to shape a new identity for society as a constructive part of Nature. This approach is both ethical and optimistic. And it is, by now, a necessity.

Gioia Gibelli

The landscape yesterday, today, tomorrow: between ethics and aesthetics

It is an endless cycle. Humanity changes the landscape. The altered landscape suggests new needs, opportunities, inventions, and modes of behaviour, which modify the landscape in turn. In this continual interaction between nature and culture, the humankind has learned from landscapes – dynamic containers of apparently boundless natural resources – how to satisfy its own material needs. Adapting itself to specific local characteristics and taming nature in accordance with them, it has found stimuli and opportunities to develop its own spirituality and creativity, which it has used to uncover new immaterial and material resources, stemming from the diversity of landscapes.

The landscape, a multiform, multidimensional and multiscalar entity, has been defined in dozens of ways, and not just in recent times. The term landscape itself has different etymologies in European languages, which reflect the variety of interpretations of the world between latitudes and from era to era. The meaning of the word for landscape is generally linked to the relationship between populations and the places in which they live – words like *land*, *pays*, and *paese* – which also implies a greater complexity.

The 20th century, when means and references changed as a result of the technological advances made by society, saw the emergence of a great wealth of thought about the landscape and its meanings, complexities and methods of study. Following this, in 2000 the European Landscape Convention provided a definition recognised on a European level: in short, the continual interactions between nature and culture are the driver of the co-evolution of landscapes, a process that began with the appearance of the human species on the face of the Earth and has continued through a stratification of the natural and anthropic changes that have taken place. It is no coincidence that the landscape has also been defined as 'the interface of resources', underlining the very close relationship between the changing 'needs' of the humankind and the management of the resources that have made human life possible. Examples of this are 'traditional rural landscapes' or 'cultural landscapes', an expression of the identity of different communities. These are generally considered 'beautiful landscapes', ones that have emerged to meet precise needs, 'taking advantage' of the availability of what is known today as 'natural capital'.

In the modern era, the high capacity for the processing of these resources, permitted by the widespread use of the energy obtained from fossil fuels, has led to an astonishing acceleration of these changes. This has now overtaken the time needed by biological elements for adaptation and brought about such profound alterations in the environment and the landscape that, since the 1980s, we have begun to speak of a new geological epoch, the Anthropocene. This new geological epoch has at its centre a single species, *Homo sapiens*, which by its activities has succeeded, through territorial, structural and climatic modifications, in influencing geological as well as sociological processes. This has resulted in the formation of a globalised aesthetic of the environment, strongly influenced by the most 'familiar setting': the urban landscape in which 70% of the population of Europe lives, with similar styles of life and patterns of behaviour.

Contemporary landscapes are the product, therefore, of a kind of divorce: humankind on one side, nature on the other. Art too has noticed: the works from painter Shelley Heffler's series 'Anthropocene 2016-2018' represent this complexity in an effective way by introducing the theme of fragmentation into the artistic image, one of the new characteristics of contemporary landscapes, and not only in so far as the physico-biological and environmental aspects and those of biodiversity are concerned. It's an endless cycle: this fragmentation has found its way into people's minds, into their thought and language, into ever more sectorial disciplines, education, and public administrations that, as a result, are less and less suited to handling complexity.

The new landscapes of the Anthropocene are having a profound effect on the shaping of the individual and of the society of the future, creating new needs and dependencies, ideas and modes of behaviour, new aesthetics, and ethics. Today the planet needs care. If the human species is going to prosper on Earth in the 21st century, it will be because we have finally understood that a new model is needed: from using the planet to taking care of it, to maintain the complexity of ecosystems and resources that has permitted humanity to appear on the Earth and to satisfy its needs.

This way landscapes of the Anthropocene, with their domesticated nature of green and blue networks, can acquire new, profoundly ethical values: those of sustainability, of the common good in our ever more crowded cities, of improvement in the quality of urban life and in people's well-being, of the 'right to reside freely in any place', of supporting the coexistence of increasingly diverse and numerous communities, of the ability to make use of and enjoy the fluidity of green spaces, in contrast to the rigidity and predictability of the grey structures of a globalised world, partly as a means of learning to deal with uncertainty. This opens a theme of choices, which pertains to a cultural and ethical process that ought to go hand-in-hand with the processes of transformation of landscapes and of a society, but that in reality struggles to find the collective awareness needed for a profound understanding of its value and, therefore, the reasons of the conservation of nature in urban landscapes as well. This is risky: an increasingly 'urbanised' population tends to make choices that go against nature, further accelerating the process of degradation of landscapes and their components that is already underway. In doing so people are unwittingly contributing to the unsustainability that we are seeing, but that we are unable to turn into a stimulus to take a different course from the ones we are currently following.

Contemporary cities are ever greedier for energy, but less attentive to the stock of information underpinning the evolution of landscapes which, like the gene pool of an organism, guides the paths of development and suggests suitable structures and configurations. Cities have an increasingly bigger 'need' for green and blue networks to boost their resilience, i.e. their ability to adapt to change, and their appeal, which depends not solely on the built environment, but also on the system of landscapes the city is part of. Hence the aesthetic and cultural components of the landscape are closely connected not only with nature, but also with the ethics that have always influenced the choices of transformation of landscapes. Therefore, ethics seem inseparable from discourses on the landscape and nature with a view to ensuring a sustainable future.

What might then be the aesthetics of the landscape in the 3rd millennium? It is an aesthetics that completely integrates the needs of nature, and thus of sustainability; an aesthetics nurtured by an ethics shaped by an awareness of human responsibilities towards the Earth, towards nature, towards the humankind itself and people's freedom to create their own landscape, while taking care of all landscapes, including the ordinary and degraded ones. An ethics that implies a conscious aesthetics: if sustainability is based on the renewability of the resources utilised, but we are not aware of what it is that nature needs to renew itself, it does not seem possible to attain that sustainability. Given that most of the population is concentrated in cities and that it is there that decisions which affect the whole territory are taken, cities are playing a role of growing importance in each of the three cornerstones of sustainability – social, economic, and environmental – that are essential to a sustainable future.

The main question today is the need to see the landscape as a pillar of urban sustainability, in sector research as well as in planning. Thus, it becomes indispensable to aim for a rebalancing of the urban metabolism, since cities, as dissipative systems that eat up resources, can and should become places that cut waste and produce their own resources, reducing the flows of energy and material that go in and out of them. Green and blue infrastructures, planned through the development of nature-based solutions suited to local landscapes, have a critical role to play in improving the quality of landscapes and human well-being, as well as the ecosystemic services that are performed by them. Services that emerge as a new model to represent the value of nature: a 'bridge' between economy and ecology, going back to the original meaning of the word economy that derived from *οἶκος* ('house') and *νομος* ('management'), i.e. household management.

Ecology is also an important tool today, an interdisciplinary subject fundamental to tackling the themes of the sustainability of cities and landscapes, of their role in the management of resources in general, as well as social justice and global change, by working on the integration of ecosystems into urban life. Urban ecology is now the frontier where ecologists can promote the interface between science and policies aimed at achieving local, regional and global sustainability, and planners can come up with landscape designs that shape the processes necessary to life.

Given the complexity of the management of the landscape today, the exchange of ideas and the work carried out in conjunction with the social system and decision-makers become an element essential to the creation of new landscapes, to the durability of the actions undertaken and to the development of a regenerative model of informed and active communities. And just as a good research piece, in today's tangible design activity, in-depth study and dissemination of a multidisciplinary work methodology is an important aspect of fostering a strategic perspective that integrates the long-, medium- and short-term objectives which projects and interventions can refer to.

There is still a long way to go, even though the sensitivities of planners, local operators and researchers are increasingly focused on finding different approaches that will allow new solutions to be explored.
The fact remains that today it is becoming more and more necessary to learn to move in an open and synergetic way, fostering a dialogue between ethics and aesthetics, as well as between technology and technique, towards a well-being once again centred on the existence of an ecosystem in which nature and human beings are integral and integrated parts of the same environment.

Emanuele Bortolotti

The Right to Nature

Manifesto for a new urban landscape and its care

How can we explore today the renewed and ever greater need for a dialogue between people and nature? What role do landscape designers play and in what way can they stimulate, facilitate, and support this dialogue? Analysis of the state of our cities and the guidelines for the development of new paradigms for the creation of an urban landscape on a more human scale have led us to the conclusion that an increase in the presence of nature in the built fabric is a true 'right' of the city dweller, on a par with the primary ones to health, education, housing, sanitation, food, and so on.

It is out of this vision the title of this volume has originated, whose content can be likened to a sort of 'manifesto' that is intended to make a contribution to the development of the future agenda for the government of the city: planning regulations and norms of interpretation for interventions, agreements between the public and private sphere and the means of planning and managing the evolution of the non-built urban fabric.

It is important to stress that terms like 'sustainability', 'reuse', 'regeneration', 'biodiversity', 'urban ecology', 'urban forestation' and so on, widely used and at times abused, undoubtedly represent the indispensable premises and contents of any new initiative. However, they often ought to be made clearer and expressed more precisely in different situations, and above all it is necessary to check whether they correspond to the real outcome. Unfortunately, though, there is much less talk of the 'management', 'maintenance' and 'monitoring' of interventions, where there is often a glaring deficiency in both the public and the private sphere, even in many exemplary interventions. Yet these factors are part of the paths we will have to take in the near future.

After the difficult years of the pandemic, a new awareness of the complexity of our cities has emerged. This new element is having a radical effect not just on urban planning and social policies, but also on people's expectations, the real-estate market, the transformation of places and the multiple supply chains involved in the process of urban transformation. It is clear that there is a new collective openness to the idea of the return to nature and the joy of outdoor living. Emerging from the confinement of the home and breaking down the barriers of the dense city to re-establish and enjoy a relationship with the natural element, without prejudice to primary needs, is today one of the values that is most closely identified with an improvement in the quality of life and in psycho-physical well-being.

This phenomenon and this clear impulse can be discerned above all in those who live or work in medium-sized and large urban agglomerations, where the effects of climate change are felt more strongly than elsewhere. The city has reached the greatest degree of overbuilding possible and is seeing a high level of social privation and widespread physical and psychological discomfort. It is no longer just a matter of curbing traffic problems, improving the quality of the air and urban sanitation, fighting decay and mitigating a pace of life that is hard to bear. What is needed is a general readjustment of the setting in which we live, through as great a naturalisation of the urban fabric as possible. Only this can set off a chain of positive changes that can bring about a true raising of the quality of life.

People's generic desire for more spaces set aside for nature, especially where residential areas are concerned, was already a discernible phenomenon and one that was extensively exploited for commercial purposes in the property sector and made the focus of simple political demagogy. But that demand is now experiencing a surprising and unexpected acceleration, under the impetus of the period of forced confinement to our homes during the pandemic, but also and above because of greater awareness of the climate emergency. These two factors have prompted all of us to take another look at the paradigms that governed life and coexistence until just a short time ago, and fostered a new consciousness of our personal needs and those of everything we hold dear. Running, strolling, lying on the grass, leaning against a tree trunk, looking at the sky, watching the flowers bloom and passing the time outdoors with family and friends, or perhaps fitting out a small balcony, terrace or porch in which to relax or work enjoying the fresh air and the view: these are things that have begun to sink into our innermost thoughts and reawaken dormant needs.

A change of perspective on the context

According to the researcher Stefano Mancuso, who for years has been investigating the behaviour of plants and looking at human beings' relationship with nature, the urban population in this country spends about 80% of time indoors (homes, workplaces, schools, healthcare facilities, shopping malls, etc.). A much higher proportion than in Northern Europe, even though the relative mildness of the climate might suggest the opposite. It is an alarming figure if we think that it is now scientifically proven that the environment is very often more polluted in our homes than outdoors.

Studying the dialectical relationship between humankind and nature, however, is not a passing trend or something generated by the market. Already in the 1970s and '80s, in fact, several distinguished scholars had clearly demonstrated people's primary need for this connection: the biologist E.O. Wilson argued that human beings have a genetic requirement to feel in harmony with nature and the psychoanalyst and philosopher Erich Fromm had coined the term 'biophilia' to describe the instinctive attraction that the human being has to nature. To these considerations we should add that life in the open air, which almost always entails movement and physical exercise, has a great influence on the physical and mental health of the individual. Therefore, vegetation and nature, seen as providing an opportunity for movement, should not be thought of solely in terms of beauty and amenity: nature is also well-being, perhaps one of the most effective means of preventing mental and physical illness.

However, why is that the presence of nature has such a positive influence on human beings? How can it at the same time make people feel good, calm them down, improve their health and the outcome of hospital treatment, boost mood and concentration, facilitate and favour socialisation and raise the quality of housing? It is now an established fact that contact with the natural world and vegetation considerably diminishes stress and malaise, generates psycho-physical well-being, and improves the intellectual powers and social skills of the individual.

In addition, nature has numerous direct and positive effects on the environment in which we live and is extraordinarily resilient. In fact vegetation, and especially trees, through leaf respiration, photosynthesis, and the shade they generate, notably cool the air, reduce levels of particulates and polluting gases and protect us from the sun and noise. This is true not only for trees but for all plants, even invasive species, and weeds, which are able to adapt to polluted urban settings. For this reason, they can be considered as a necessary resource for the survival of our environment.

A new urban landscape and new formulas of life outdoors

In light of the above, it is clear that those who work in landscape have a great responsibility to operate in the most correct and effective way possible; this involves interpreting reality to open up new scenarios, while finding their way between complex regulations and government policies through a vision that has to be completely new and constructive. A thorough study of the relationship between the individual and nature is essential, moving between urban and domestic life, and a 'biophilous' attitude toward design aimed at the creation of a diffused landscape made up of spaces and systems of greenery, adopting an ecosystemic approach rooted in *nature-based solutions*. In parallel it is necessary to apply all the technical expertise and experience needed to create pockets of nature into the dense urban fabric, taking advantage of the numerous opportunities to insert greenery between buildings and multiplying the many corners of unexpected nature (small gardens, conversions of courtyards into planted areas, green roofs, roof vegetable gardens, hanging gardens, green light wells, façades and blind walls covered with plants, pavement-gardens, etc.). It is a 'special' kind of nature that implies knowledge and technical skills to choose the right plants and keep them alive and growing in cramped spaces and in close contact with buildings, often in constrained conditions. The results can be surprising if we rely on the amazing energy and vitality of plants, managing their growth so that they offer us the best without coming into conflict with the built environment.

The values of landscape design should turn around the need to bring nature more and more into the everyday life, offering maximum accessibility and inclusivity where open spaces are concerned. This means promoting healthy lifestyles, well-being, socialisation, and culture, making the most of the natural anthropic characteristics of places and their influence on people's sense of identity as well as urban potentialities and imagining open spaces that take care of their human and animal inhabitants.

The paradigms of a new urban ecology

The new challenges regarding the improvement in the liveability of urban settings require a continual modification of the applied paradigms. Some possible actions, or approaches, are today an integral part of projects more attentive to the environment, such as limiting the amount of land take for new constructions; counting on regeneration and reuse of what already exists; depaving and increasing, where possible, the permeability of the soil and the use of rain gardens, which favour the drainage and temporary storage of excess water, the result of changes in the pattern of rainfall; fostering biodiversity and the planting of more trees.

Other actions are more necessary than ever to guide the planning and ensure the best results are attained. Actions that span the different scales and themes of design, from the strictly environmental to social and economic ones. They include establishing continuous and interconnected systems that go beyond the vision of a nature divided into separate parcels (urban greenways, green belts, protected cycle and footpaths); integrating and expanding the presence of accessible green areas, suburban farming and forestry, with routes for sustainable mobility and channels of heat mitigation and the free flow of air between city and countryside; promoting urban wilderness schemes and urban forestation; creating water retention areas; supporting and fostering new modes of participation in nature, such as 'shared gardens', flower beds laid out on pieces of public land connected with residential buildings and other ways of involving the population and voluntary organisations in order to encourage users, over time, to look after and protect public space and to develop a greater sense of ownership and responsibility; research into and establishment of new forms of constructive collaboration between the public administration and the private sphere in the realisation and subsequent management of green areas.

Thinking about a new urban ecology signifies integrating all the aspects of our urban and extra-urban habitat and getting them to work in synergy with one another.

Which 'right to Nature'?

The 'right to Nature' as we conceive it is much more than an objective. It is a true intergenerational pact. This investment in the future requires a bold change of pace supported by a new perspective that reflects on what spending time in the open air and in contact with nature really means today.

Just as has happened with alternative sources of energy, actions to combat global warming or measures to increase the birth rate, nature should be seen as a way of reconnecting people with the city and an important factor in re-establishing a balance that cuts through society.

Themes like the 'regeneration of the outskirts' cannot disregard the need for major investments in urban nature that help to turn the 'ugly' into the 'beautiful', and that offer city dwellers opportunities and pleasant and comfortable places in which to encounter nature, as a point of anchorage for a new sociality. The efforts to set in motion a process of such scope ought to be supported using private resources in schemes of urbanisation, but also by ways of providing incentives and tax relief for good practice. The fact is that municipalities do not have sufficient means to sustain by themselves the burden of urban transformation linked to the expansion of areas set aside for greenery and their maintenance.

Finally, we need to look at the work done by residents' associations and the volunteering sector, which are increasingly often taking over degraded areas to carry out projects of urban *greenification*, creating a new identity for the neighbourhoods. A beneficial practice that ought to be studied and adopted by all town and city councils.

Paolo Palmulli

Diffused landscape

People's well-being at the centre

This book begins as a manifesto and then unfolds as a path to be explored, rather like what happens in a park when, after passing through the entrance, we feel compelled to look for new sights, opening ourselves up to new ideas that evolve over time, changing and growing, but which are only possible because the right seed has been sown. It is necessary for us to understand, interpret and design the new settings of coexistence and life in contemporary cities through a new relationship between humanity and nature.

Ever since the drawing up of the European Landscape Convention in the year 2000 and its subsequent modifications, as well as the more recent institution of a National Landscape Day in Italy on 14 March 2016 and of the Council of Europe's International Landscape Day on 20 October 2017, the definition of landscape as a setting whose qualities exercise great influence over people's lives seems to have become well-established. We consider this concept of landscape to cover all the more or less urban spaces in which we live, however exceptional or degraded, and above all the ones we experience on a daily basis.

The inclusion of the whole of the territory in which we live is a clear recognition of the extent to which any space is able to establish complex relations and interconnections between places, such as urban and rural areas or central and peri-urban ones, and the consequent need to ensure that every individual is able to enjoy the quality of the urban landscape.

Starting from this premise, for many years we have been drawing on the concept of 'diffused landscape' in our work. For us this represents a vision, an approach, but also a methodology that defines a more pervasive presence of nature. A nature that is integrated into the urban built environment, located in its gaps as well as in larger spaces, so as to create hospitable places, not only in parks and areas set aside for vegetation, but also in all those niches of open space that play a part in people's daily lives, becoming a new asset for our cities. An approach that sees the landscape as a great interconnected network, able to generate the sort of environmental and ecological continuity that can foster and protect the wealth of biodiversity, even in an urban setting. A precious resource open to all that contributes to the benefits of living in a city; one that is commensurate with the everyday needs of thousands of people and is able to shape attractive, useful and functional spaces in the urban landscape.

In the face of the great changes our cities are going through, it is growing increasingly important to develop the capacity to look closely at the resources at our disposal and to make the most of them, learning to recognise what is part of our daily experience: educating ourselves in beauty, learning to distinguish between excellence, acceptability and degradation. We cannot be complacent, and it is necessary for us to pursue an ideal of beauty that can satisfy all our senses, one that is able to generate a fulfilling landscape, pleasing even to contemplate: creating a memory of places that can endure in time.

We must learn to reutilise what already exists: it is there that our future lies. It is necessary to reconnect people with nature, even in the most complex, compromised and varied urban settings.

The diffused landscape relies on the qualities that derive from coordinated urban, landscape and strategic planning; qualities that do not stem from single episodes or exceptional facts. To attain these objectives, it is indispensable to have careful planning in order to free spaces from concrete beforehand and favour environmental continuity: an integrated project that brings a range of specialists together around the same table, including architects, civil and road engineers, landscape designers and agronomists, as well as administrators and politicians. The inhabitants also have to be involved, through participatory processes that boost the value of the intervention and ensure its duration in time.

Nor can we ignore, especially in this country, the growing role of the private sector as a promoter of major urban transformation. It can act as a guarantor in the creation of spaces devoted to nature through its interaction with public oversight: in this dialogue we must look for possible ways to improve the quality and increase the quantity of open spaces. This option can be made feasible by the establishment of agreements between the public and private spheres, sometimes on an experimental level: from the opening up of private spaces to public use to the assignment of areas to be dedicated to the landscape and provisions for their long-term maintenance, in an increasingly hybrid approach to the management of public space.

The work of clients, designers and contractors, together with that of the administration, if carried out with commitment and dialogue, allows every problem, desire or necessity that emerges to be interpreted in the best way possible, facilitating the integration of the landscape into the whole of the work, along with every single detail. The upshot is a project that can really be shared by all.

The aim of this attention is not to set in motion a virtuous process for its own sake, but to shift the focus onto the key factor in any transformation of the landscape: people. The experience of the diffused landscape, in fact, has a profound effect not just on the individual, but on the community as a whole. It changes the collective experience and the way in which people see themselves and relate to the world around them. Carrying out a project of diffused landscape with natural elements signifies giving an identity back to a place, offering its inhabitants a new vision of their everyday existence. It is a question of undertaking simple and precise actions aimed at creating pieces of landscape within the urban fabric, ensuring their success and making them an integral part of the city and of people's lives.

Good design of spaces devoted to nature presupposes making wise, well-considered choices, picking carefully the place, the soil, the technical and technological solutions and the most suitable plants and materials. It also means making provision, right from the first phases of conception, for an adequate programme of maintenance that will permit the preservation of that quality over the course of time, adjusting and adapting the project to changes in needs and the extent of use.

Fundamental, too, is the organisation of means of participation, whenever possible in the early stages of conception and certainly in those of implementation and once the project is underway. Here it is necessary to rely on environmental education as a way of raising awareness and building a sense of belonging to the place, so that the residents become its protectors, watching over it and taking care of it.

The greatest challenge is maintaining the quality of the public space over time to achieve valuable results after carefully creating the works. It's indispensable to supervise the spaces, prevent problems, and be able to act in a targeted and effective manner. A good landscape generates a bond, and those who live in it tend to respect it. With these assumptions, maintenance becomes more sustainable.

The landscape is alive, transforms itself, and evolves. The plant elements grow, they may have different needs over time and can be used differently. It's necessary to initiate medium and long-term management and maintenance processes, with the awareness that they will have to be reviewed, specified, and improved. This evolving and open approach to change allows for versatile spaces ready for uses and functions that can accommodate new future dynamics.

The various actions that need to be carried out in an area in order to create a diffused landscape can take the form of innovative and stimulating solutions. This may entail a willingness to look at unconventional proposals and ideas, at the stage of both the conception and the development of the project, as well as during the process of its realisation, with the introduction of specialist works supervisors (a role that did not exist in Italy until a few years ago). True experts on the landscape can guarantee an excellent result from the viewpoint of the realisation, maintenance and management of open spaces as well.

Thanks to this methodological approach, requiring integration of the disciplines, responsibilities and scales of reference, it is possible to intervene in the dense and intricate mesh of the urban fabric of contemporary cities, acting in all the possible spaces. Out of it can come a widespread system of vegetation and minute connections that will comprise and establish a synergy between all types of open space, whether public or private. These spaces need to be made more and more accessible and permeable, demolishing boundaries that can represent a limitation on the potentialities of a place: this ability to connect up urban open spaces through a network of multiscalar continuity of nature is the essence of the concept of diffused landscape.

To integrate spaces devoted to nature as well as possible into the fabric, we have to look for them in the places where public space becomes the backbone of the new landscape and establishes a natural and harmonious relationship with private space, without any leftover corners or marginal areas, and above all without any break between public and private works.

A good relationship between public and private space does not find expression solely through visual or aesthetic elements but extends to deeper layers of city life: the parameters become the correct use of spaces, urban order and functionality, in addition to ecological and environmental benefits. The diffused landscape leaves behind neither waste nor residual spaces, stripped of any role, but is a unitary conception of many harmoniously inserted details. In the general context every well-placed element improves the appearance, perception and function of the other spaces. The private intervention cannot be made correctly without taking into due consideration what happens outside its bounds. It will be exactly those elements and those references that are going to further enhance the intervention.

In this way it is possible to overcome boundaries and be ready to look beyond them, continuing to expand without trauma and dysfunctions, connecting up with the scale not only of the immediate surroundings, but also of the district and the city. It is a crucial element in a complex territorial system, where local features are interpreted and made the most of by inserting them into a broader unified framework with which we can identify. We have a right to landscapes that are more open, easier to make use of and accessible to all, without overlooking the indispensable value of their beauty, a quality that is essential to the achievement of a true diffused landscape.

Our cities are the work of different generations and civilisations and are a demonstration of the extent to which time is a fundamental component of the urban landscape. The stratification of centuries of history has come down to us as an amalgamated and cohesive cultural product, a fabric of places in which people recognise themselves as a society, even though those spaces have to be adapted to the new needs that every age brings.

In this climate of continual social transformation of uses and habits, the only constant references are space and nature: all the rest must be left free to evolve and change over the course of time. A good project should lay the foundations for the creation of a place that will acquire a symbolic, functional and environmental value of its own. A value that will increasingly be recognised by future inhabitants, in such a way as to supersede traditional references and provide a new interpretation of the city.

Over the course of the last century, the dialogue between the built environment and nature has not always been a fruitful one. Themes like ecology and the protection of the environment have emerged in response to a heavy-handed, problematic urbanisation that still persists, but that is finding more suitable responses, drawing on a greater understanding and one that is rooted in history. Certainly, the day-to-day needs of contemporary society are different now, as are those of the spaces representing that society. Often it is a question of necessities that cannot be foreseen at the beginning of a landscape project, but the latter has the great luck of being able to count on nature's capacity for change, its ability to adapt and be modified on the basis of just these vagaries.

In the urban context, in which today in particular the forces that bring about those frequently not fully controlled or planned changes are diverse and often insistent, with repercussions on social and economic dynamics, the 'right to the city, the right to nature and to culture deserve this bet on our future', to quote the words of Salvatore Settis.

In this framework there is a possibility of improving our settings, of establishing a dialogue between the forces at play in the name of the well-being of both people and the environment. The designer can and should sow the seed from which a landscape will grow that will tell the story of its community, including the emotional sphere, inviting everyone, as city dwellers, to take care of it and to carry on with the creation of a place in which to live well, to live better, something which is the right of us all.

Alessandro Frigerio

Urban landscapes of the near future

Gradients of nature, continuity, solidity and beauty

Every day, those who take on the task of transforming physical space are faced with the challenge of imagining the future we are going to live in and finding the best way to fit themselves into the processes that determine what the world will become; all while trying to do so from a perspective of their own and using a particular imagery, expressions of a cultural position. For those who call themselves landscape designers, the concept of nature is central to this work of transformation, as it puts humanity back within a broader frame of reference that pertains to the reasons and risks of its very survival, as well as to the essence of its way of life, in harmony with its fellow creatures and the planet.

The events of the last century have led to profound changes in this relationship between humanity and the Earth, accelerating the impact of human domination over nature and opening a complex reflection on our responsibilities in the epoch of the Anthropocene, while climate change is making its effects felt in the daily lives of the inhabitants of every part of the world.

According to the figures given by the United Nations in support of the 2030 Agenda for Sustainable Development, over half the world's population (it will be two thirds by the end of 2050) now lives in cities: urban settlements that take up only 3% of the Earth's surface, but are responsible for 75% of carbon emissions, contributing significantly to climate change and putting the planet's ecological balance at risk.

Urban and metropolitan territory, therefore, is the main field of research in which planners can act in order to try out ways of restoring balance to the relationship between anthropisation and natural resources.
A balance that entails asserting and promoting the need to defend the right to the protection of nature – and therefore to a healthy and sustainable environment in which to live – as well as the right of access to that nature – in terms of fruition, multisensory perception, and education – as a right to landscape viewed from a cultural perspective.

The challenge we face in restoring balance to our anthropocentric vision of things is a complex one, especially when viewed in relation to very different climatic, social, and economic situations. However, nature is already a growing presence in the urban spaces of many cities around the globe. It is possible to discern in this process two general trends with respect to motives and modes; trends which need to be seen in synergistic relationship with the raising of public awareness linked to international agendas and to the emergence of needs, desires and demands on the part of urban populations.

A first tendency, result of the quantitative character of the modernist rational-comprehensive approach to city planning and stoked by contemporary performance-oriented culture, has transformed the generic emphasis on 'greenery', as a functional standard (with the requirement of a certain amount of 'greenery' per inhabitant), into more or less sophisticated parameters of environmental impact: from simple counting of the number of trees planted, for example, to calculation of the amount of carbon dioxide they store and the hope that it will be possible to come up with a way of quantifying the ecosystemic services they provide in economic terms. An increase in the presence of nature in the city is justified and promoted based on those services.

A second tendency, connected instead with the way in which the allure of nature – or more banally of anything that is 'green', including imitations made of plastic inasmuch as they do not have to be looked after – has become in vogue. Indeed, it can be said to have turned into an obsession in the sphere of urban and property development and its related marketing campaigns, verging in some cases on greenwashing. If in the 20th century the cities of the future were imagined, from *Metropolis* to *Blade Runner*, as hyper-dense and ultra-technological machines, today such prefigurations couple 'smart' digitisation with luxuriant nature, sometimes condensed by the algorithms of artificial intelligence into a curious ecological cyberpunk.

Both tendencies present the risk of excessive simplification, banalisation, or manipulation, but constitute potentially significant means of raising public awareness of the environmental challenges we are facing. They can also provide important opportunities for landscape designers to win recognition of their key role in the processes of urban transformation, with a necessary call for an increase in that awareness and an assumption of responsibility.

If nature really is the solution to all our problems, as many argue, it seems opportune to ask, adapting a famous quip by Cedric Price on the role of technology (already regarded in the 1960s as the panacea for every challenge of the near future): okay, nature is the answer, but what was the question?

Landscape design, in fact, operates through the integration of aesthetic-formal, ecological-environmental and socio-functional aspirations, with weights assigned to these three different factors that vary in relation to the contexts of reference, the specific requirements and the aesthetics of design. However, the balancing of these aspirations is crucial and, especially in urban settings, has to be connected with people's needs and desires. The risks of predominantly technical-performative or aesthetic and decorative approaches can be summed up in terms of their ineffectiveness in shaping places since they neglect the cultural and human heart of the matter.

It was Cedric Price again who stressed this aspect back in 1977 when he wrote, on the subject of the presence of nature in the city, that people need trees and trees in the city need special care, but in order for them to receive that care a sense of belonging has to be developed:

a bond that is forged when these trees are located in a place that people love. And this happens if the trees become part of these people's lives, generating social or sentimental spaces to visit, to explore, to dream about, to design.

A tree is never just a means of providing shade and purifying the air or a decorative object. A good landscape design, in harmonising the complexity of the relationship between city and nature, has to be able to construct places, i.e. create spaces that, by layering and intertwining meanings, are part of the individual and collective life – in the past, present and future – of a community. In this way it becomes possible to bring a conscious relationship with nature back into the everyday experience of the city, since its value as a common asset is recognised.

The responsibility of the landscape architect – in close coordination with the disciplines of planning, architecture, and urban design – does not lie, to cite the cultural position adopted by Ernesto Nathan Rogers regarding the role of the designer, in an 'abstract and eccentric utopianism', but in aiming for a 'utopia of reality' that signifies 'projecting the present into a possible future'. So, it is necessary to think about how urban landscapes are really going to evolve in this closer relationship between city and nature. By trying to imagine the cities of the future in terms of this effort to instil new meaning, we can hypothesise three lines of approach to the research and the work, identifying them by means of three keywords/concepts.

Firstly: continuity. Landscape design, in the wake of Charles Waldheim and James Corner's reflections on the concept of landscape urbanism, is taking on a structural role with respect to regeneration and urban development, playing an ever more significant part as support and matrix for processes of reassembly of fragments of urbanization and open spaces. The landscapes of the near future will have to meet a decisive challenge in the search for continuity. This finds expression in the need, starting out from a thorough knowledge of the contexts, to work towards the repair and strengthening of urban socio-ecological networks, giving concrete form to the design principle of diffused landscape often referred to in this volume.

Making the most of open spaces and the existing natural heritage, in combination with the introduction of different types of landscape capable of establishing new functional and/or ecological connections, can result in the creation of a multiscale and multifunctional infrastructure. At the same time, this infrastructure performs an ecological and environmental service for the urban metabolism and provides a system of public assets and spaces of cultural identification: a structure indispensable to the survival of the cities of the future and their inescapable public dimension and to the well-being of their inhabitants.

Secondly: gradients of nature. The presence in the city of forms of nature that we connect with the aesthetics of the wild is increasing, following on from the European experiences of the last thirty years that have sprung out of the reflections and projects of Gilles Clément and Piet Oudolf on the reintroduction or recreation of wilderness. It is something, however, that has also become necessary as a response to the impracticability of the intensive and onerous maintenance of public spaces. This is a question that will become increasingly critical with the expansion of urban nature and that is already leading to a shift in paradigm from maintenance to management (monitoring, tending, experimentation), as Annalisa Metta has argued in her recent studies of the rewilded city.

In constructing the systems of continuity referred to above, the urban landscapes of the future will be characterised by the simultaneous presence of innumerable landscape-based modes of interaction between human beings and nature, with different levels of intensity, naturalness, domestication, integration and care, along a gradient that will extend from the wild to the technological – from the rural meadow to symbiotic biophilic architecture – developing synergistic relationships for the strengthening of biodiversity, the production of ecosystemic services and improvements in the access to nature for all urban populations. A greater level of education and awareness with respect to this great variety in terms of meaning, aesthetics and value will be both desirable and necessary.

Thirdly: solidity (and beauty). The future by its very nature is uncertain and landscape design requires the setting in motion of lengthy processes. In the imagery of the city to come there are landscapes of prefiguration (as Michel Desvigne defines them) and intermediate kinds of nature for the experimentation, reinvention, and appropriation of spaces, as well as resilient and adaptive landscapes able to go along with or resist changes in climate and in other factors. Any project for the future, however, must reckon with the idea that the landscapes we design have to take on board an aspiration to and principle of solidity. Paolo Villa, founding partner of AG&P, in his book *Solido come un parco*, considered this solidity to be the result of a design able to create places robust enough to be subjected to appropriation and care, and therefore invariable and structuring with respect to developments in urban planning, construction, or socio-politics: common assets to be defended and protected. This aspect of solidity also results in a less ephemeral or trendy kind of beauty, an ethical beauty that is associated with ideas of justice, inclusivity, accessibility, and democracy and that needs to be pursued with conviction and determination, in every form and at every level of design. This also affects the way it interfaces with any new technological or digital tool that is going to be used to assist designers in the future.

Viewing landscape design from this perspective signifies turning it into something that can contribute to the processes of negotiation involved in urban transformation, something that can be achieved by supporting the need to make intergenerational pacts on behalf of those yet to be born.

Already today, the adoption of these three lines of approach is making it increasingly necessary to plan the city in a systemic rather than a sectorial manner, protecting, reinterpreting, or inventing urban places with a greater awareness of the role that nature can and ought to have: an exploration that leads to the imagining of new typological figures for open spaces. While expressions like tree-lined boulevards, waterfronts, and public parks and gardens have been part of the vocabulary of city planning since the 19th century, the opportunities offered today by research into green and blue infrastructure or other kinds of nature-based solution (NBS), along with the technological advances that have allowed the presence of nature in highly anthropised settings, are leading to the definition of inventive forms of design. Forms that are able to reconcile aesthetic, ecological, economic and functional aspirations: new kinds of places awaiting ideas and names that will give them (new) meanings and a systematic character. This will in turn make it possible to exploit and re-signify the vast urbanised territories of the established cities and metropolises that are expanding in many parts of the world.

A research that also opens up a significant opportunity to de-Westernise landscape design, superseding and supplementing the historical typologies of European origin with a transcultural multiplicity of experiments centred on nature in accord with specific contexts. It is a question of shifting – in the words of the British geographer Matthew Gandy – from the 'urban culture of nature' to the 'culture of urban nature'.

This change of perspective, associated with the three paths of assuming responsibility described – which represent a partial view of a complex and evolving scenario – can contribute to the construction of an ethics and aesthetics of urban sustainability in the present and the near future, fundamental characteristics of the idea of a right to nature that lies at the heart of this book.

Green and blue infrastructures

The landscape of green and blue infrastructures: the natural matrix of urban systems

For much of the 20th century, the phenomenon of intense urbanisation of large areas of the planet turned more or less anthropised landscapes into mere land to build on, run through and fragmented by infrastructures of every kind. As well as becoming firmly established in the predominant technical culture of town planning, the concept of 'green' as the background colour to urban sprawl lodged itself in people's imagination: 'green' as the generic common denominator of any kind of open space that was spared, be it a central reservation in a road or a playground, a residual or obligatory allotment to meet standards of the quantitative type. While policies and schemes for the protection of biodiversity have focused predominantly on the maintenance of spaces and species of particular value in protected natural areas, in urban and peri-urban areas anthropic pressures have resulted in the degradation and fragmentation of natural habitats, with numerous consequences that have contributed strongly to the current climate crisis, the reduction in biodiversity and the impoverishment of the soil, and to the creation of situations of water and food as well as socio-economic and cultural insecurity. The change of paradigm that has progressively emerged in recent decades has led to the existing urban natural heritage as well as the potential one – disused industrial sites, vacant lots, ruined buildings, abandoned land and residual spaces – and to smaller-scale and more fragmented areas – residential gardens, urban vegetable gardens, green roofs and walls or balconies – being regarded as a possible single integrated natural system: a diffused landscape suited to guaranteeing and supporting biodiversity, generating new urban ecologies within the dense fabric of the city and its bordering areas, in contact and connection with rural ones.

Today, thinking about such integrated and continuous systems, able to offer environmental qualities and benefits for the community and for nature, represents the vision at the root of the concept of 'green and blue infrastructure' (GBI), an approach to the conservation of biodiversity based on the maintenance of ecological networks, ensuring the survival of animal and plant species and providing multiple ecosystemic services to urban communities.

In the establishment of GBI as a complementary asset to traditional 'grey' infrastructure, the delivery of services constitutes a fundamental element, since integrated and continuous ecological systems themselves function as infrastructure. Unlike many grey infrastructures, however, typically oriented towards a single, specific purpose, natural systems carry out a range of functions simultaneously; functions that are of benefit to people, ecosystems, cities, and the planet, and that reconnect human beings with nature. GBI provides ecosystemic services and essential benefits to the urban population that are environmental, economic, and socio-cultural. Commencing with the restoration and maintenance of soil quality, regulation of the microclimate, reduction in pollution, drainage of rainwater and support of food production, they extend to recreational and cultural services of which city dwellers make direct use, and which are requested and enjoyed at a local level. Multiple indispensable benefits guaranteeing the quality of life in the present and the future.

This ability to be naturally multifunctional makes GBIs extremely valuable and the effort that goes into their creation – through works of urban *mending*, renaturalisation, integration, appropriation and upkeep – is amply repaid over time, even though the investment required, in both economic and socio-political terms, can entail long timescales and the forms of financial recognition of the services they supply are much debated, but still far from achieving convincing modes of implementation.

For this reason, GBIs, understood as multifunctional socio-ecological systems, have become today an essential instrument of urban and regional planning, from the small to the large scale. Protecting the environmental integrity of the places in which we live requires a physical continuity of the system of open spaces and ecological connections that establishes a direct connection between urban parks and protected areas on a larger scale. In this way networks are formed that are capable of structuring development and/or urban regeneration in a way that ensures the protection and enhancement of natural resources.

The challenge for those who design landscapes is to understand how to create these connections, establish this continuity and imagine – often invent – new figures of landscape able to marry the different expectations placed on GBI.

AG&P greenscape has been taking on this challenge for years now, promoting a methodological approach that treats every project, on whatever scale, as part of a wider and more complex system of landscape, to make the most of open spaces as components of a diffused landscape that is in the process of coming together. Each project examines the potential for the repairing and priming of socio-environmental infrastructures, with repercussions and benefits extended to the context. This means starting out from the anthropic and natural characteristics of the location: the structure of the landscape of GBI is always an interpretation of the geomorphology of places, their history, and the pre-existing natural features.

This reflection has been developing for almost thirty years due to the studio's involvement in the project for the Centroparco in Segrate, and has continued through several projects of diffused landscape, such as the more recent Parco del Paleoalveo in Bergamo or the Parco Arborea in Monza. It has also been part of collective and interdisciplinary efforts of a more wide-ranging nature, as on the occasion of the drawing up of the Regional Strategy of Sustainable Development of the urban system of Savona, in Liguria.

These are significant examples of the shared planning and/or implementation of a socio-environmental vision of infrastructure in close interaction with the various actors involved, following, or envisaging the evolution and realisation over the course of time of pieces of green and blue infrastructure with a high value in terms of ecosystemic services and socio-economic impact. The Centroparco project got off the ground at the beginning of the 1990s with the aim of reclaiming a quarry that was winding down its operations together with all the adjoining areas, in the vicinity of the centre of Segrate (a small town on the outskirts of Milan).

Left: study view of the Parco del Paleoalveo in Bergamo.
Below: Crescenzago Park in Milan.

On the previous page: aerial photo of the Centroparco and sports area of the Istituto Comprensivo Schweitzer in Segrate.

Left: a view of the Cascina Merlata neighbourhood park on the outskirts of Milan.
Below: view of the park of the new Milano 4 You neighbourhood in Segrate.

On the following page: map of the Territorial Strategy of the city of Savona, a scenario for a socio-ecological network that supports adaptation to climate change and the increase of urban biodiversity to improve the quality of life of citizens; highlighted are the main areas for the regeneration of public spaces through some pilot projects.

This was seen as an opportunity to turn them into a large system of public spaces equipped with facilities and integrated with the neighbouring private residential gardens.

Today it covers an area of over a hundred hectares. Peering into the future of these spaces, residual negatives of the processes of urbanisation of the diffused city, the approach to their landscaping has seen them from the outset as potential spaces of quality relationship, able to impart a structure to the loose-knit urban fabric characteristic of peri-urban areas and thus to offer a new mental map of places special to their inhabitants.

This operation of restoration to the community, which combines the intentions of creating equity and beauty, has found concrete expression in an integrated vision of the landscape that regenerates a portion of territory to offer a wide range of ecosystemic services with repercussions for the context of Segrate, as well as for the entire metropolitan area.

And it is this bent for the construction and enhancement of a cross-scale and intergenerational environmental patrimony that has made possible the continuity of the project and the support it has received over time, increasing every day the significance – which goes well beyond the immediate benefits, however important – of the use of the areas progressively placed at the disposal of the community.

The sharing of objectives and the cooperation between the different actors in the area have made possible the gradual implementation of the initial vision of the creation of a peri-urban metropolitan centrality that was not based on building or carried out for commercial reasons, but rooted in the landscape, and with a blue heart. The urbanistic and planning instruments promoted by the local authorities of Segrate have been put in place deliberately to meet the different political aspirations of the town councils that have succeeded one another over the course of time. This has been done in dialogue with the landscape designers and the private actors, without deviating from the overall vision of the project and putting its success in jeopardy.

An important experience that has brought different players around the same table, in a relationship both direct and delicate in its balancing of the public vision with the needs of the industrial activity undergoing decommission and of property developers, who have believed in and strongly supported the project from the outset.

A significant challenge for the planners too, who have found themselves dealing with a palimpsest of anthropic (agricultural and industrial) and natural features to interpret and give new meaning to, in part through the invention and combination of figures of landscape that perform at one and the same time a civic and an ecological role.

The Centroparco today is an important ecosystem, still in the process of completion, that can become an attractive public space both at the local level and at the metropolitan one, as a node in a broader expanse of open space, making the most of all the systems of landscape, from green to blue.

The same approach has been taken to the project of the Parco del Paleoalveo in Bergamo, a city that has always paid attention to the preservation of its peri-urban areas, choked as its surroundings have been by the disintegration of the agricultural landscape under the pressure of urban sprawl and infrastructural development.

Betting on a gradient of naturalness that favours an idea of diffused landscape and proposes a model of more integrated and sustainable urban growth, the project envisages the environmental reclamation of an area on whose edge is planned a new intervention of urban transformation. This will be done through enhancement of the traces of landscape and the existing environmental heritage from a perspective of protection and consolidation, favouring a balanced opening to the public.

The presence of water in the area, an ancient palaeochannel with wetlands, traversed in turn by a system of irrigation ditches, is the characterising element of the project, and one of the principal resources to be developed as blue infrastructure. The aim is to make the most of the memory and history of the place, its potential in terms of the ecosystem and biodiversity, its role as a public space of connection with nature and in the building of a greater environmental awareness. A project emblematic of how city and nature can be integrated in a stretch of rarefied urban fabric.

The Arborea project interprets the theme of the diffused landscape, combining private residential spaces and a system of public and natural spaces, in the peculiar setting of a bend in the river Lambro, in Monza. As part of an urban planning scheme of predominantly residential character that will take the place of a disused industrial complex, the landscaping project has an important part to play in giving a special place back to the community, while providing the opportunity to reconsider a set of green and blue infrastructures of particular significance for the whole river system and the surrounding area. The aims can be summed up in the improvement of the area from an ecological perspective, in keeping with a new experimental plan of management of the watercourse that has envisaged the renaturalisation of its banks, and in the creation of a new park, public spaces and foot and cycle paths connecting the city and the open space. The design of the gardens of the residences, both communal and private, as well as the greenery on their balconies, completes the system of landscaping, from the green and blue infrastructure of the riverside park that works in relation with the Lambro to the flower box on the balcony, from the public to the private. The project proposes the environmental reclamation of the area through an intervention of renaturalisation integrated with the open spaces of the new district, leaving at the same time room for the river and its dynamics of expansion.

The landscaping project for the new district proposes, in fact, a gradient of naturalness that overcomes the sharp separation between

San Giacomo
Monticello
Pertini School
Priamar
Climate adaptation
Biodiversity
Heritage

city and countryside through an idea of diffused landscape that offers a model of more integrated and sustainable urban development.

Green infrastructure was defined by the Communication from the Commission to the European Parliament in 2013 as 'a strategically planned network of natural and semi-natural areas with other environmental features designed and managed to deliver a wide range of ecosystem services'. It is modelled like a promising means for developing the new strategies needed to favour biodiversity and for adaptation to and mitigation of climate change. Integrating it into planning on the different scales of the city, the territory and the landscape should become a necessity and prerogative of any intervention in physical space.

Consistently with this approach, the studio's thinking on these themes has also given rise to tools of strategic planning of greater complexity, such as the Regional Strategy of Sustainable Development of the urban system of Savona, in Liguria. This tool, built together with a multidisciplinary group based on an urbanistic, environmental, and socio-economic analysis backed up by a process of listening to the inhabitants, suggests a reorganisation of open space and the public patrimony in order to implement a socio-environmental network supported by the exploitation of a system of civic nodes, i.e. public buildings treated as defenders of the adjacent public open space. Thus, the strategy consists of a regional scenario that represents the potential grid of green and blue infrastructure and of a constellation of specific planning operations that concern the civic nodes and their open spaces. These are actions designed to trigger urban and regional transformation, with the aim of mitigating the risk of environmental and social vulnerability and improving the resilience of the area. The regional strategy for Savona is a major landscaping project for the city that combines an enhancement of the historical and cultural heritage and the stock of public housing with an increase in biodiversity and measures of adaptation to climate change, in a new geography of places in which democracy, quality of life and beauty come together and provide the conditions for sustainable urban development.

View of the Centroparco in Segrate, with the existing pool in the background.

Centroparco, Segrate, Milan

Located in the middle of the fragmented archipelago of urban settlements that make up the municipality of Segrate, just a few kilometres from the centre of Milan, the Centroparco is a truly green work of infrastructure that covers over a hundred hectares, a set of landscapes that integrates city and nature. The almost thirty-year-long process that led from the first idea to the current situation – and that will continue in the years to come – has its roots in a principle of generational equity, intended as the capacity of a community to build up and defend a patrimony of natural and cultural resources able to nurture the growth of future generations. The project entails the long process of transformation and reclamation of a disused production site and the surrounding areas, commissioned and supported collectively by the public administration and private bodies. At its base lies a vision of integrated landscaping that sets out to regenerate a piece of territory to mend the system of relations of a strategic portion of the Milanese peri-urban area and offer a range of ecosystemic services to the local community and the entire metropolitan region. Inside it, nature has been enhanced supporting it by intervening in a careful and precise manner, permitting the different species to find their right habitat again, and, at the same time, integrating various facilities, spaces for play, sport and relaxation, gardens, foot and cycle paths and housing. At the centre, a large expanse of water characterises the whole area, reclaiming and adapting the spaces of a former quarry so as to give it back to the people of the city as a landscape resource.

Dialogue with the team

Emanuele Bortolotti, Paolo Palmulli,
Sofya Dolgaya, Barbara Frangi,
Alessandro Frigerio, Pierpaolo Tagliola

The roots of the story of Centroparco go all the way back to the 1990s, when, thanks to an overarching vision of great importance which was the result of the dialogue between public and private actors, the decision was taken to create a large urban park on the outskirts of Segrate, reclaiming the areas occupied by a quarry that was winding down its operations. A complex project that grew over the years, adapting to and setting out to meet changing requirements resulting from the evolution not only of people's needs but also those of nature itself.

Paolo The story of Centroparco is one of common growth, shared first of all between the public and private promotors, but also in dialogue with the local community, who has grown fond of the idea over the years and continues to be interested in its progress as if it were a place for the family, an outdoor extension to their homes. The ambition was to give people back large natural spaces that for years had been inaccessible or unusable. To attain this objective, it has been necessary to plan its growth step by step, adopting a sustainable strategy able to gradually make new portions of the park usable each year. Today Centroparco has some developed areas already in use by the community, others that have been approved or are under development, while sections are still awaiting the imminent end of the quarrying activity.

The basic idea is to look at the landscape as an element of quality that has to be spread to all scales of the project. All while considering the area as a complex system of landscape and infrastructure.

Emanuele The concept of *diffused landscape* is the basis on which the entire Centroparco project has been conceived. We consider every single space devoted to nature to be an integral part of a single grand system of landscape, whether we are talking about the gardens of private residences, areas allocated for public use or public space and the park in its entirety. Each of these interventions connects with other projects promoted by the municipality of Segrate over the decades; projects that contribute to shaping an ever more sustainable future rooted in the quality of the landscape. From the Chilometro Verde to the Ciclopolitana and the extension of the M4 line of the Metro: all this integrates in the Centroparco. It is clear that the scale that needs to be looked at is the local one, but it is also that of the metropolis, in the attempt to establish visions and above all come up with more open solutions in synergy with the surrounding region.

How has this effort of listening and action towards the area developed?

Alessandro The park has been the subject of various research phases, projects and urban plans, but also of moments of listening and interaction with the various municipal administrations that have succeeded one another, and with the citizens, with a particular focus on the youngest, who have been involved in imagining the future of certain areas.

0 50 100 200 m

These activities contributed, in turn, to identify the project's potential, allowing us to build the vision that today sees the area transformed from a place of production, inaccessible to citizens, to an ecological and social centre open to all, capable of connecting parts of the city that were previously separate. This immense area of about ten hectares has obviously been divided into lots, in order to be able to follow each transformation more closely and in a synergic and integrated manner. The knowledge acquired over time has allowed us to test certain solutions, listen to the territory and respond promptly to its evolving needs. The master plan we have drawn up is designed to accommodate the evolution of nature, as well as changes in the needs and desires of its users, while maintaining its structure in terms of ecological changes and connections. In general, the project's synergetic objectives are, on the one hand, the reconnection of the different neighbourhoods with each other and with the park, with the promotion of cycle and pedestrian mobility, and, on the other, the conservation and improvement of natural elements for the development of biodiversity and the defence of ecosystem services for the benefit of the city, bringing nature closer to and integrating it into the daily life of citizens, respecting it.

The area of Centroparco is, in fact, part of a whole set of complex transformations, brought about to turn it into an ecosystem service thanks to its multifunctional environmental network.

Paolo Yes, certainly. This vision extends along three main themes: environment (air, water, soil, and biodiversity), production (sustainable economy, locally sourced food, energy, ideas, recycling) and socio-cultural (memory, sport, education, participation, care, housing, meeting, sharing). The updated master plan, with its unprecedented vision that revises and completes the earlier scheme from 2006, organises a series of processes and ideas that are being put into effect currently, which will eventually serve to boost the connectivity and attractiveness of Segrate and its park at a metropolitan level.

Where did this strategic role of centrality on a number of scales, suggested also by the name of the project from its first conception, come from and how was it interpreted in the master plan?

Alessandro The centre of the socio-ecological system described by Paolo, which is the heart of the Centroparco and its characterising element, is the body of water left over from the quarry's mining activity. A network of green spaces and connections branches from this centre, energizing the surrounding urban fabric. Its ability to constitute a centrality is due to its exceptional character in relation to the landscape system of the local area, now largely compromised. Despite the paradox that it is an artificial lake, this body of water is the pivot around which the entire project revolves. This is also the origin of one of the most important challenges of the master plan. How to design a large open space that is a remnant of a compromised agricultural landscape, transformed by industrial activity and besieged by the pressure of urbanisation? The project seeks to incorporate these conditions by enhancing the traces of the agricultural landscape, supporting the spontaneous phenomena of naturalisation of the area and introducing some equipped spaces typical of urban parks. A mosaic in the making that is also a laboratory for understanding how to transform large peri-urban open spaces that have remained unproductive (both in economic and ecological terms) in order to give them back to communities as systems of relations and multifunctional green systems.

There are a number of areas and spaces in the park that are dedicated to people's activities and reflect an approach to the search for a dispersed quality in order to make the landscape more accessible to all, in both the public and private space.

Paolo Centroparco represents a wide-ranging vision, which consists of a mosaic of projects that collectively make up the overall picture. In the past few years, we have designed and followed the realisation of the areas closest to the centre of Segrate, dealing with urban spaces, road spaces and an initial large portion of the park, overlooking the lake.

On the previous page: general volume plan of the Centroparco.

Right: view of one of the Centroparco's paths.
Below: view of the lake in the park's recovered former quarry.

Map of the environmental system of the central-eastern part of the Milanese metropolitan area. The blue heart of the Centroparco is a dimensionally and symbolically significant presence in the peri-urban strip between the historic core of the city of Milan and the agricultural landscape to the south-east: a significant node in a potential metropolitan socio-ecological network that interweaves the green and blue infrastructures envisaged by the various municipal and supra-local planning instruments, identifying new centralities with a landscape vocation.

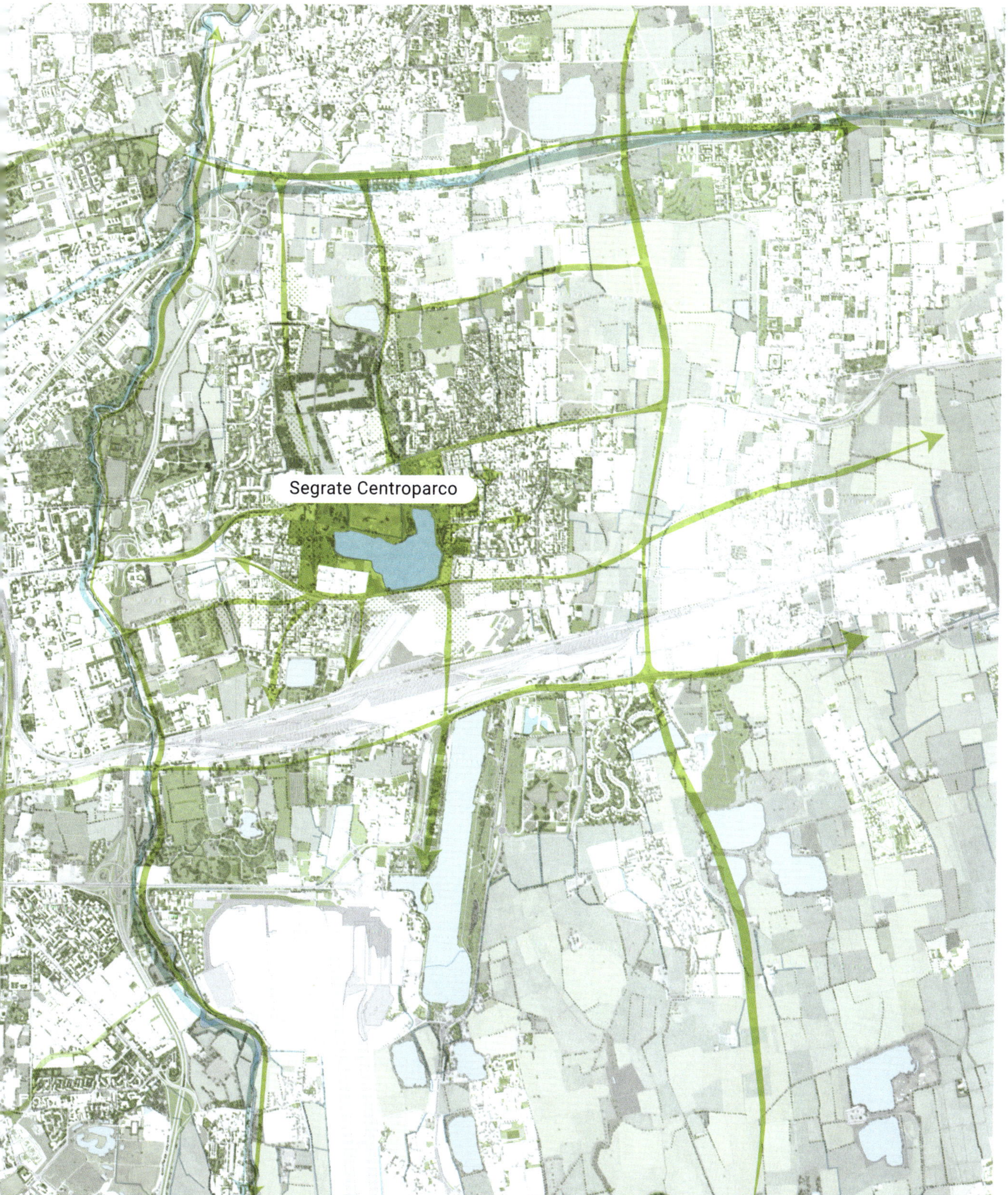
Segrate Centroparco

On these pages:
studio cross-sections for the new topography of the western area of the Centroparco: a synthesis of functional and ecological-environmental scenarios.

Left: one of the paths within the Centroparco.
Below: the view from the terrace overlooking the lake formed from the former quarry.

On the following pages: a view of one of the park's routes and the lake.

We are now focusing on the design of the specular areas, while waiting for the industrial quarry activity to be permanently decommissioned, so that we can proceed with the completion of the cycle and pedestrian ring that surrounds the lake and is the backbone of the system of paths. We have renamed it 'Corso Centroparco' and it represents the *fil rouge* of all these areas, a path that is very versatile and safe, with slow lanes for those going slowly and fast lanes for those in a hurry, full of spaces for stopping and resting, access to facilities and activities, without ever interfering with its main function, to allow all users to cross the park and access the various neighbourhoods of Segrate, in an easy, convenient way, immersed in nature. Each of the areas that make up the mosaic of the park has its own prevailing vocation, with attention to maximum accessibility and inclusiveness, providing equipment and facilities for all ages and all needs, distributed in environments with different degrees and characters of naturalness. The private areas facing and in relation to the park are also part of this mosaic.

Sofya As Paolo pointed out, the key aspect of the Centroparco project is that the quality of landscape is found in all its parts, even in the private areas of the residences, underlining the concept of a diffused landscape as an added value of the scheme. In these years, during which we have been dealing with the public spaces of Centroparco, we have had the opportunity to design some private open spaces of the residences that overlook it or are close to it, also thanks to the urban mechanisms that link private investments and the realisation of public facilities that support the progressive completion of the Centroparco. These were very important opportunities to build the synergy we are talking about in terms of diffused landscape. A way of landscaping even condominium gardens, with the same care and attention that is put into creating a private and more intimate garden, at the same time assuring quality spaces for living and ecological continuity to environmental systems, from which the entire community benefits.

Barbara This theme acquires a fundamental value, especially after everything we went through during the pandemic. Never before as in recent years have we been able to appreciate how much nature is good for our lives, starting from the point of view of personal psychological and physical well-being, both in the case of direct or even just visual enjoyment of nature on our doorstep. But the ability to produce well-being, especially in open urban contexts such as that of Segrate, has many facets. For example, the presence of nature is able directly, and indirectly, to reduce the temperature even by a few degrees, a sort of natural air conditioner based on the capacity for shading and leaf evaporation.

All this is obviously also through an increased biodiversity guaranteed by the widespread presence of nature.

Pierpaolo Certainly. Even in a small, shared garden it is possible to apply strategies that are fundamental to the conservation and fostering of biodiversity. There are times when small actions can change the population of living creatures in a garden to an incredible degree. The planting of a mixed hedge instead of a monospecific one, pruning at the right moment so as not to disturb nesting birds, combining evergreen species with perennials that have long flowering periods, perfect for pollinators. The consideration to design and the role of care that accompany smaller projects such as community gardens, make these small spaces interesting boosters of biodiversity when placed in relation to and in continuity with larger landscape systems.

Water too Is of fundamental value to the growth in biodiversity: it makes an important contribution to the diversification of both flora and fauna.

Pierpaolo People have no idea of how much life can turn around a single body of water, from the large lake reclaimed from the quarrying activity, the central area of the park, to the ponds in the gardens of the private residences. At all scales of the project, from that of the park to that of the small, shared garden, encouraging the growth of spaces devoted to nature represents an act of awareness and gratitude. But then, that's exactly what biodiversity is: the natural expression of a delicate balance. Making sure that it can be maintained and enjoyed by all is certainly our responsibility, and even more so today than in the past. A healthy and bold vision of the city of the future has to include the integration of a diffused landscape, as added value for the coming generations, to be handed down as a concept and as a means for the pursuit of high-quality projects.

It can be said that the main reason why it has been possible to develop a project as complex and wide-ranging as that of Centroparco over decades is precisely a shared vision of the landscape as an indispensable resource.

Alessandro That's right. The value of Centroparco lies in a very ambitious, yet very simple landscape vision: regenerating a portion of land to provide a space accessible to all that is pleasant to enjoy and offers a multiplicity of ecosystem services to the local community and the entire metropolitan area. And that is beautiful, of course. Often, when we talk about it, we tend to take it for granted, but aesthetic quality is crucial, also for the processes of appropriation and care that can ensure the long-term survival of a landscape. Fortunately, Centroparco has already begun to offer natural sceneries that amaze and engage those who visit it. What animates our project efforts and what we try to convey to all those involved in this process, is that the multiple benefits that the project can offer concern environmental, ecological, social, economic and cultural values, which are indispensable for ensuring the quality of life in the present and especially in the future, considering the climate challenges that await us. It is this calling for the enhancement and construction of an intergenerational environmental heritage that has made possible the continuity and consensus for the project over time, which year after year is progressively 'liberated' and made available to the community, which in turn receives it with amazement, a little impatience, and appropriates it.

Centroparco, Segrate, Milan

Public planning as a tool to protect and develop the environment

Conversation with

Paolo Micheli and **Francesco Di Chio**
Mayor and Deputy Mayor
of the municipality of Segrate*

What are the programmes in course, or that are going to be developed in the future, for a greener Segrate, one that is more attentive to the environment and the questions of the ecological transition?

Paolo Micheli We are continuing with the protection of the area that we launched with the plan drawn up in 2017, giving a million square metres of open space that had been slated for urbanisation back to the town. In the new municipal planning tool that we will be drawing up with residents over the course of the next few months, there will again be a call for a stop to land take and for policies attentive to the environment, climate change and the ever-growing cost of energy. When we took part in COP26 in Glasgow in November 2021 we made it clear on what side we stand. We want to become a model of sustainability. The Segrate model will be that of a town in which public transport will be more efficient and convenient, due to the arrival of the Metro, where the amount of unurbanised land will increase rather than diminish: thanks to the Chilometro Verde (Green Kilometre) project we will be removing three kilometres of asphalt along the Cassanese, a busy road leading into the town, where we are going to plant a tree for each inhabitant to oxygenate the air we breathe.

*Interviews published in the insert OASI GREEN, issues nos. 1 and 3 of the daily newspaper inFolio

How was the experience of COP26 in Glasgow? What points in common emerged with the policies of other towns of the same size? What good practices did you talk about on that occasion?

Paolo Micheli Only three towns and cities in the world took part in COP26 in Glasgow. We are very proud to have been one of them. We talked about what we are doing to combat climate change and what we are going to do. The Chilometro Verde project went down very well, since it is an initiative of environmental restoration that bucks the trend: instead of building, we are removing concrete that is already there and giving land back to the citizens to improve their quality of life. We have calculated that in the area of intervention the reduction in the number of vehicles in transit will also cut the emissions of CO_2 into the air by 60%.

The Chilometro Verde, which is integrated with the Centroparco, represents an incredible resource not only for the town of Segrate but also, looking at a broader field of action, for the whole of the Metropolitan City. How and when was this project born?

Francesco Di Chio The project emerged in parallel with that of the *Viabilità speciale*, or 'special road system'. With the opening of this new bypass which will carry most of the through traffic, the four lanes that the Cassanese has now will no longer make sense. Whence the idea of depaving part of the road, creating a green corridor leading to Milan with cycle paths and new opportunities for recreation and socialisation for the people of Segrate deriving from the unification of the Centroparco, the Parco Alhambra and the Golfo Agricolo.

Together with a few other Italian municipalities, Segrate has set up a department of ecological transition. What does it do?

Francesco Di Chio This delegation brings into focus the goals that we want to achieve to improve the quality of our lives. We have initiated a change with respect to the policies of development of the area, and it is up to us now to strengthen this approach of sustainability. This delegation is a recognition of the work done and an indication of the road to follow.

The theme of urban growth is an important one to tackle. What are the policies in place and the modes with which the municipality interacts with private investors?

Francesco Di Chio Segrate is a modern place and one that looks to the future. It is open to private investments that bring prosperity, work, and new opportunities. Over the years Segrate has grown in an uneven manner and today is still paying the price for the economic and territorial damage resulting from those planning decisions. Anyone who wishes to invest in our town today is perfectly aware of our objectives and the ways in which we intend to develop the place. There is only one watchword for us: sustainability.

The participation of local people plays an important part in public policies. It was with this in mind that the Segrate CityLab was set up. How does this platform work?

Francesco Di Chio The Segrate CityLab is a workshop of ideas where it is possible for people to examine the interventions of public interest that we will be working on in the coming years. Our frantic lives make us look at the things to be done today. It is more difficult to look ahead at what has to be done tomorrow. But with Segrate CityLab we can take a leap beyond everyday actions to have a long-term vision of our town, which will be more friendly, modern, secure, and united in sport, in culture and in nature. Anyone who wants to participate can do so through the website and we are open to all contributions.

The Centroparco project was launched many years ago now, and over the course of time has been developed with great foresight by a succession of local administrations. Could it also be described as a model for the way that the public and private spheres can work in synergy to improve the quality of life and of the town?

Paolo Micheli The Centroparco, and now our project of the Nuovo Centroparco, is undoubtedly a very positive and interesting model of collaboration between public and private. The Nuovo Centroparco is and will be the heart of the town. A place able to connect different districts that up until a few years ago were separate from one another and hard to reach. A place in which to live, meet up, practice sport, stroll and relax amidst the vegetation. A green lung just eight kilometres from the centre of Milan, a magical place that enchants whoever sees it for the first time.

Regeneration

Transforming, reusing, giving back parts of the city

Since the beginning of the new millennium, if there is one word that has characterised the transformation and urban development of the world's great cities more than any other, this is undoubtedly 'regeneration'. With the growth and consequent decommissioning of parts of the 20th century city – whether former industrial sites or underdeveloped areas, between the edges of others already built, or places no longer suited to a society in constant and rapid change – regeneration has been the engine that has changed the DNA of contemporary cities.

Often the outcome of public initiatives (in the rest of Europe, mostly) or private initiatives (in Italy, these are more likely), the aim of urban regeneration programmes from the outset has been to increase the 'city effect' in order to regain a sense of urbanity and improve citizens' quality of life, while also recovering compromised environmental situations. These programmes have identified strategic directions and generated conditions to strengthen and improve social capital and attract economic resources to convert public and private areas for transformation and reuse through various forms of intervention. These areas might be decayed historic centres, obsolete residential and ex-manufacturing districts and neglected portions of the landscape. While there are undoubtedly positive aspects of change and improvement in the quality of urban space obtained in the first regeneration initiatives, with the beginning of the new millennium, and following the financial crisis of 2008 and the consequent reduced capacity for public spending, considerable evolution has taken place in the transformation processes of some parts of the city. Certainly, the advent of financial capital in the dynamics of investment and urban development has determined precise paradigms in configuring regeneration projects to achieve guaranteed success, with success in most cases. These paradigms at first often led to a certain uniformity in the character of the solutions realised, building an international image set concerning regeneration processes that was uniform and regular, spectacular and with appealing architectural projects to attract more and more users and financiers.

It has taken several years and many changes, also in the ways of experiencing urban space, for the paradigms of urban regeneration to evolve, due to changing conditions. Today it is possible to experiment with design proposals that are more closely linked to the local context and above all to the communities of citizens that those spaces will have to inhabit, in the name of an identity of the interventions that is increasingly integrated with the peculiarities of the place and the presence of nature.

And if on the one hand private investor pressure has been the driving force behind some of the largest and most important urban transformations in global cities, on the other hand the free initiative of citizens has also emerged in an increasingly significant way, which has found in the paths of urban regeneration a valid tool to give new life to disused, abandoned spaces waiting to be transformed, either temporarily or permanently, through collective and participatory actions.

Two aspects of urban regeneration, the one more related to financial investment and the one promoted directly by citizens, show how important it is to focus on the quality of open, common, shared spaces, bringing into dialogue the urban landscape and its inhabitants. Precisely thanks to the experience gained over the years of countless urban regeneration projects, we can now highlight the existence of a structural gap: the city cannot always keep up with the 'times' and speed of the social and physical transformations that affect it. In the absence of conscious direction and a timely and adequate design response, the city sometimes suffers from planning inertia, a lack of adequate redevelopment measures, and a rapid extension of the residential, commercial, industrial as well as tourist fabric that is inattentive to public space and landscape. With population growth concentrated in large metropolitan centres, then, the complexity of the new urban scenarios is reflected in the increased difficulty of both understanding and describing the connotations of the contemporary city, and of thinking of new policies capable of grasping the signs of change and managing its various aspects. Above all, cities that are historically lagging in the adaptation of public spaces, services, and collective facilities are today unprepared because they cannot keep up with the speed of change.

It is, therefore, crucial to recognise the changing demand for public spaces, which corresponds to evolving patterns of life, to analyse the potential of spaces awaiting transformation in the social and environmental transition towards more sustainable future cities.

In this dimension of urban regeneration, which alternates and articulates between the pressure of the drive of private investment capital on the one hand and the speed of societal changes on the other, the overlapping of public and private interests regarding the quality of public space determines new forms and processes of transformation of parts of the city, attentive to the issues of environmental protection, accessibility and usability of places, and the enhancement of the built heritage, not only in economic terms but also and above all from a cultural and social point of view, with a more stringent need for spaces dedicated to nature and within everyone's reach.

Nature has increasingly become the protagonist of new urban regeneration interventions, evolving from a complementary presence to a structural and integrated element of transformation processes, in a new season of interventions in which the multifunctional landscape value of open space has become a cornerstone around which projects are often developed.

In this perspective, AG&P greenscape has always interpreted the term 'regeneration' as 'transformation', 'reuse', and 'restitution' of parts of the city for its inhabitants, to improve the quality of open and built space by increasing the presence of nature, whether through large-scale private or public interventions or local initiatives promoted by citizens.

Various regeneration projects have been tackled with this approach, ranging from large ur-

Top: the project Varesina 204 | Certosa District, in Milan.
Above, left: a view of the Forgiatura | Certosa District.

Above, right: the Giardino Nascosto during the PianoCity event in Milan.
Below: images of the pre-existing site.

On the previous page: view from above of the Waterfront di Levante area in Genoa.

Top: the courtyard of the Opificio residential complex in Via Carlo d'Adda in Milan.
Above, left: view of the ARIA project at the ex Macello site in Milan for the Reinventing Cities competition.

Above, right: view of the courtyard of the office complex in Tortona district in Milan.
Below: images of the projects' pre-existing sites.

ban transformations – such as the Reinventing Cities project on the ex Macello (former slaughterhouse) area in Milan – to smaller ones – such as the redevelopment of the former Opificio in Via Carlo d'Adda in Milan – and support for citizens' bottom-up initiatives – such as the Giardino Nascosto (Hidden Garden) reuse project by a local association. All interventions in which the role of the landscape architect is increasingly fundamental in holding the ranks of the working groups, offering that ability to work on the grand scale as well as the smallest, in the ideational design phases as well as in the construction phases, with the same attention and quality, to generate landscape pieces that are connected, appropriate to, and integrated with the context.

With this interpretation of the regeneration project, the studio has developed several projects for the Genoese coastline, understood as important grafts of a broader strategic vision for the transformation of the territory through a continuous green and blue infrastructure system that is regenerating the city's waterfront, returning substantial portions of it to the citizens.

The 'Genoa system', in fact, intervenes on that stretch of the Ligurian seafront through a series of operations that reconfigure the landscape and the relationship of the territory and the city with the port and the water, a link that, in the course of local history, has not always been oriented towards dialogue and exchange, often opposed precisely by the productive functions that have defined its character of non-accessibility. Rethinking new generation interventions on these places represents a way to (re)encounter the sea and give back parts of the city to its inhabitants, configuring a true 'landscape system', with a view to an increasingly accessible and usable nature.

The waterfront represents an urban landscape system where the link with the water can combine environmental care and different ways of experiencing this special place: the ecotonal belt of the relationship between land and sea landscapes is articulated in the combination of different figures of public spaces gathered along a linear system with a vocation that is both urban and natural, called upon to fulfill different functions in the short and long term, such as the regulation of the microclimate or the management of the consequences of the possible rise in sea level. This approach interprets the waterfront not just as a simple urban area to be developed, but as an urban system of integration between city and landscape, through which to experiment and draw inspiration for a more sustainable and resilient development, without forgetting local characters and identities. Following the spirit of this systemic approach, the interventions on the Genoa waterfront have been interpreted, from the Parco delle Dune, which reinterprets the relationship with the port area to offer citizens a quality public open space, where parts of the reconstructed landscape dialogue with new equipment and services; to the Parco della Lanterna, which creates an important public park, in terms of size and symbolic value, reconnecting the city to one of its identity symbols, port lighthouse, thanks to the major infrastructure project of the sub-port tunnel; up to the Waterfront di Levante, which gives back to Genoa an area, that of the former trade fair, which has always been limitedly accessible, to create a piece of the city where nature becomes the pioneer of a new urban space, a large park that is the relational system of the new district, conceived as an urban forest of the sea, a characteristic and extraordinary element of the project.

Regenerating an urban space becomes even more valuable today in light of the strong growth pressure that large cities are under, and having to severely limit land use.

Transforming, reusing, and returning parts of the city to the inhabitants, under the banner of spaces increasingly understood as pieces of landscape and a new way of experiencing the dialogue between nature and the built environment, is undoubtedly one of the most important challenges that landscape architects will have to face shortly. Finding a synergetic way of thinking of the territory as a landscape system to reconstruct new links and development trajectories is one of the possible solutions.

The environmental system of the Genoa area and three landscape transformation projects underway on the seafront.

Parco della Lanterna
Parco delle Mura
Waterfront di Levante
0 250 500 1 2 km

Parco delle Dune, Genoa

The Parco delle Dune project, located in the final stretch of the Prà stilling basin, 720 m long and with a surface area of 40,000 sqm, transforms a mitigation structure of the port activity, giving the inhabitants of Genoa a highly inclusive gathering place with a clear and robust landscape identity. A link between the city and the sea, the park is punctuated by dunes of different heights, offering an oasis for leisure and activity.

On these pages: plan, section, project view and site image.

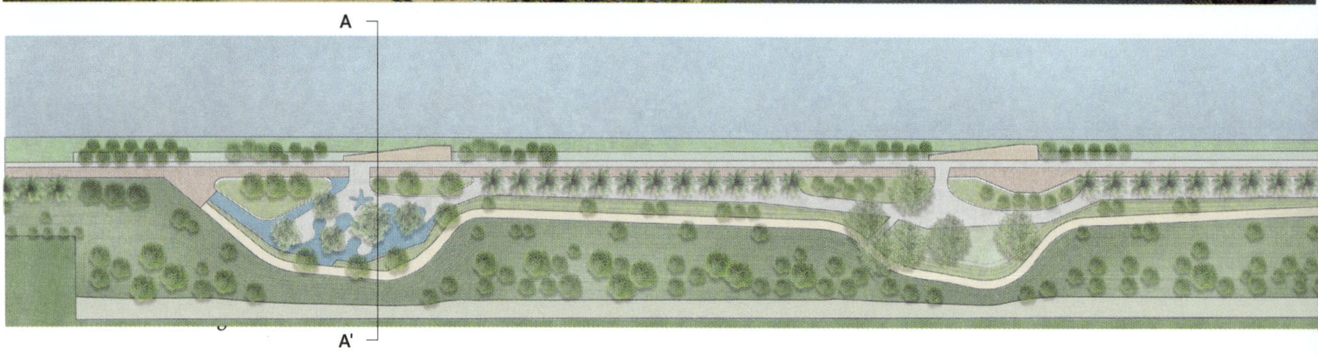

A–A'

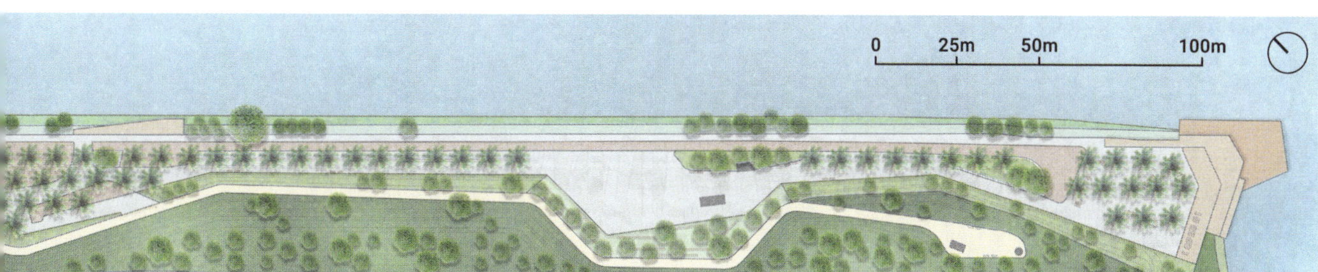
0
25m
50m
100m

Parco della Lanterna, Genoa

The Parco della Lanterna is the most significant of the interventions associated with the construction of the Genoa sub-port tunnel, a strategic infrastructural work for the reorganisation of urban and port mobility, an opportunity on the west side of the city to create a new large public space that reconnects it with its most important symbol.

Memory

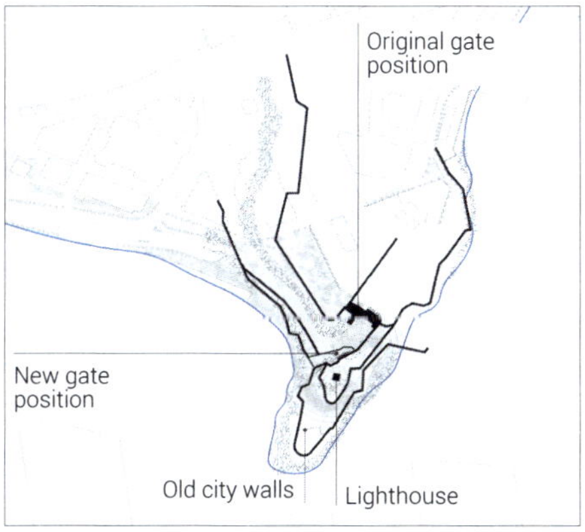

Connections

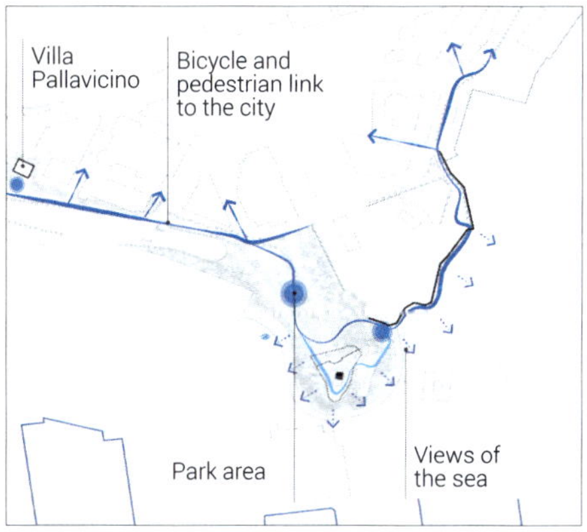

On these pages: planimetry, section, project view and image of the park landscape project.

On the following pages: photo of the Waterfront di Levante project as seen from the sea.

Waterfront di Levante, Genoa

The Waterfront project, developed by Renzo Piano Building Workshop, OBR (Open Building Research) studio, Starching and AG&P greenscape (for the landscape design), envisages the regeneration of the former area of Genoa's trade fair, facing the sea with urban and public and private port functions. These include a large urban park, a dockyard, residences, offices, retail outlets and a renovated Palasport, an indoor stadium that is now to be turned into a multifunctional building.

It is an operation of 'urban mending' that turns what used to be the rear of the port into an urban front onto the water, where Levante and Ponente, east and west, are reconnected, closing the gap between city and sea caused by the development of the port carried out after the end of the war. Conceived as a super-urban place, the Waterfront is designed in such a way as to generate a new way of thinking about a contemporary district, where nature and water will become the key elements around which the open and permeable project is developed, preserving the character of both the port and the city.

The large urban park is the most extraordinary element of this regeneration. Designed as a mineral and vegetal environment, it aims to be an experimental, pioneering urban space in Genoa, densely lined with trees, and directly overlooking the sea. It is the first portion of a public system that will gradually reconnect the Corso Italia promenade with the Porto Antico, re-evaluating the presence of the elevated highway and establishing a new relationship with the historic walls. The definition of landscape guidelines for the entire master plan, which have identified the material and vegetational abacus (inspired by the Ligurian landscape and the historical parks of Genoa) and their technical-dimension requirements, have also guided the architectural and specialised choices to ensure a high-quality open space easily maintainable over time.

Dialogue with the team

Emanuele Bortolotti, Paolo Palmulli, Chiara Battini, Alessandro Frigerio, Georgia Karsioti, Pierpaolo Tagliola

The interventions you are making along the Genoese seafront are representative of the fact that it is increasingly necessary to change our approach when tackling themes like regeneration, planning and urban design. How can the landscape help us find new ways?

Paolo In the face of the many changes we have been going through in recent years, from climate to economic and social shifts, it has proved necessary to change our approach towards design and planning. Nature plays an ever more central role in urban regeneration projects. We need to look at the diffused landscape as a system of landscapes, which generate value together. It is with this vision that we deal with the various interventions currently underway along the Genoese coast, from Parco delle Dune, in Prà, to the Waterfront di Levante project (developed in collaboration with RPBW, OBR and Starching) and the areas of the tunnel under the harbour (with RPBW). All these interventions tackle themes of urban regeneration in terms of giving back pieces of the city, enhanced through the introduction of nature, to the local community.

The Waterfront di Levante project in Genoa is an intervention on a large scale, where public space, water and nature have a key role in defining a new urban context, in which the term 'regeneration' finds a new scope. How did this project arise?

Paolo The project stemmed from a strong need for renewal of the city, and out of an extraordinary public urban vision, shared by a number of stakeholders. I call it extraordinary because with intuition and a spirit of innovation they have launched a project that holds all the cards to becoming a new model of urban regeneration.

Alessandro The Waterfront di Levante began from the vision presented in the Blueprint master plan that Renzo Piano donated to Genoa as an opportunity for the city to find a new exposure towards the sea, beginning from the trade fair area, which had been closed off to the citizens for decades. The master plan is the first element in a new system of public spaces that will be able to connect the area of the trade fair with the Porto Antico, the old harbour. A project that turns what was hitherto partially or completely inaccessible into an urban front onto the sea, placing the public space at the centre.

How has the relationship between public and private sphere been handled? And what role has the studio had exactly?

Paolo This operation of urban regeneration is a good example of public-private partnership, in which both spheres join forces to transform an area and then to manage and maintain it, raising the quality of the spaces enormously, in the short and the long term. Today there are public-private agreements that can cover up to thirty or forty years of management by a private entity, guaranteeing the best functioning and maximum results. These represent an added value for everyone, above all for citizens.

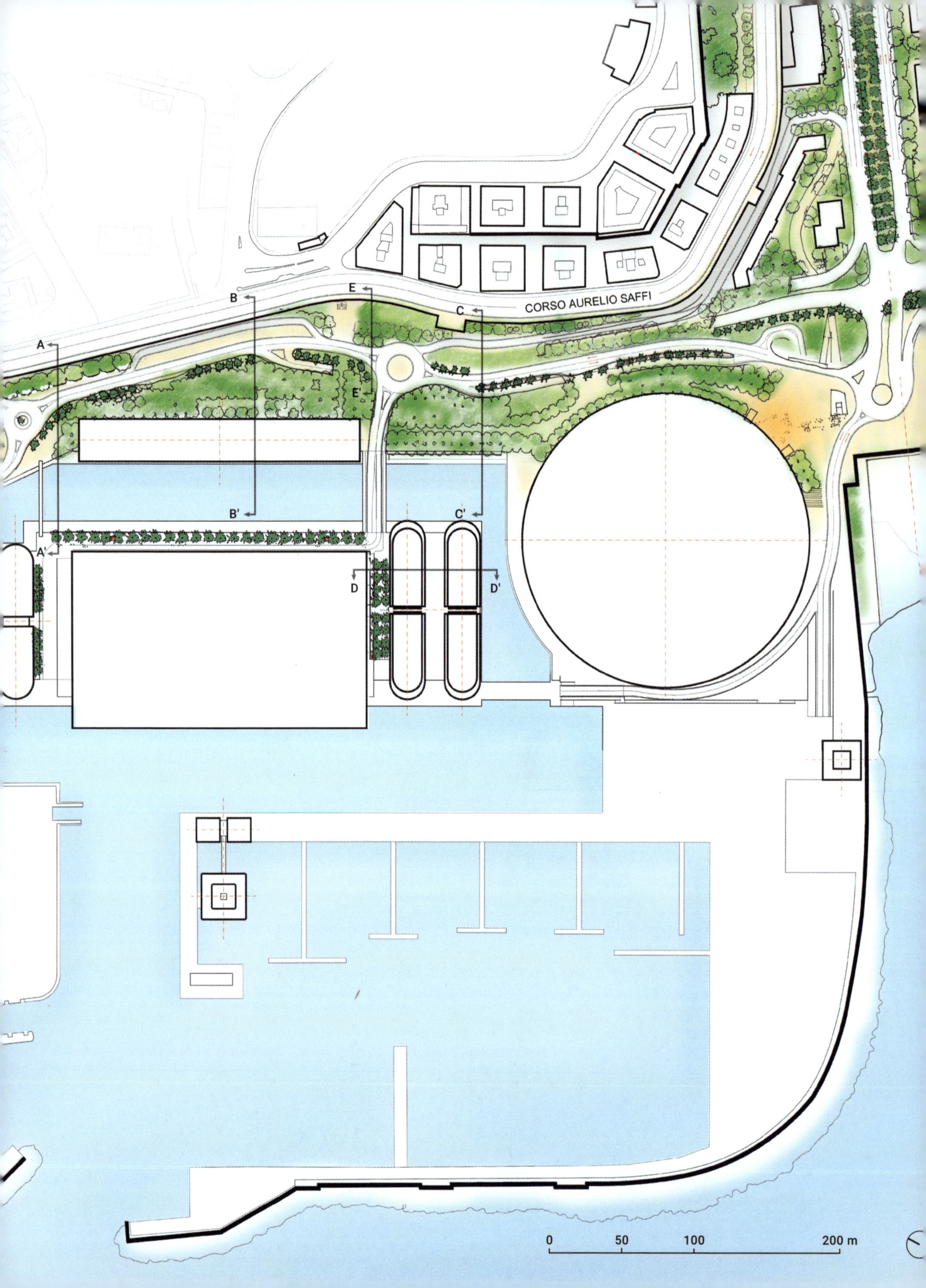

CORSO AURELIO SAFFI
A
A'
B
B'
C
C'
D
D'
E
E'
0
50
100
200 m

Left: map of the Waterfront di Levante landscaping project.

Below and on the following pages: some sections of the project, showing the relationship between buildings, vegetation, water and the old city walls.

A–A'

B–B'

C–C'

The study sections shown on these two pages illustrate the role of nature in characterising the different landscapes that distinguish the master plan, with particular attention to spaces of greater infrastructural complexity. In these cases, too, no effort has been spared to integrate a rich mix of vegetation to offer a multisensory experience to the user from multiple levels: that of the adjacent public space; of the views from above from the apartments, or from the walls; of the moving views at different speeds, from the new panoramic lift, or cars passing by on the elevated highway.

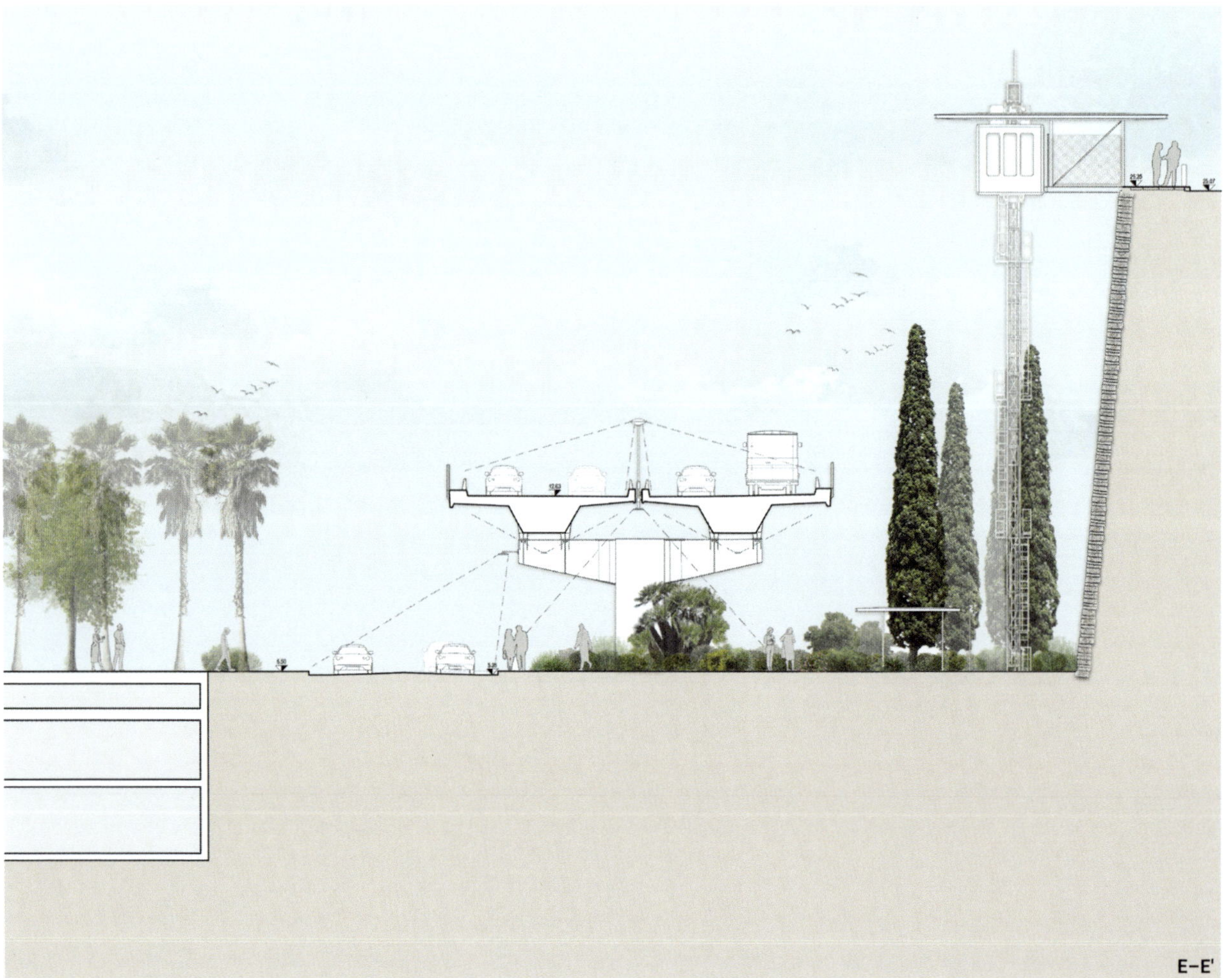

E–E'

D–D'

D–D'

Emanuele AG&P has overseen the preliminary design of all the outdoor areas of the general master plan in close collaboration with RPBW, coming up with guidelines for the development of the various lots, some of which were then designed directly by us. The landscaping system of the public space is one of the key elements of the project, connecting, in the first place, the different parts of the city that, like a hypothetical green thread, aspires in the future to link up again east and west, Corso Italia and the Porto Antico, healing the break between city and sea caused by the development of the port since the last war. The system of open space, in reality, is intended not only to connect and improve the accessibility to these parts of the city, but also and above all to provide new opportunities for people, spaces for recreation, leisure, play and sport, facilitating a new relationship with nature in a place closely connected with the water.

Alessandro The theme of giving back is fundamental to the effort to recalibrate this kind of relationship. In the case of the Waterfront di Levante area, the construction of the trade fair and the elevated motorway took the beach and the original coastline away over half a century ago, so it is not a question of giving back strictly speaking, but rather reactivating a place that allows the public to access the seafront, through the landscaping project and the elimination of all barriers, which will allow the city and its inhabitants to face freely onto the water again.

So, it will be a new district, integrated and connected with the rest of the city?

Paolo The ambition of the project, which we share, is precisely that of creating a new district, one that proposes a wholly innovative way of living on the water in Genoa. An invention that passes through the construction of an artificial plate on two levels in which public space and vegetation act as a great element of collection and union of the different parts. The most interesting aspect is in fact the difference in levels, which are 5.5 m and 1.2 m above sea level. On the upper one, continuous with that of the Foce district, is located the more urban area, with housing complexes, commercial activities and public spaces; while on the lower level there is the quay of the marina, with its connected activities. AG&P has set out to invent a new way of understanding public space – located on the higher level – that reinterprets, and updates, systems and foundations of a landscape able to stitch back together the historic and modern city, nature and the sea.

What will be the most innovative aspect of the project?

Alessandro The innovative proposal made jointly by AG&P and RPBW has been to come up with a space that did not exist in Genoa: a coastal urban park, characterised by the presence of a large forest on the sea. It is a completely new place, one that has the physical and visual continuity of natural systems, where people will be able to have an immersive experience among the trees from which the landscape springs. RPBW's idea for this place makes a highly poetic reference to *The Baron in the Trees*: it should allow the protagonist of Calvino's novel to make his way through this kilometre-long forest, from east to west, passing with ease from one tree to the next.

Paolo A forest, however, that is not closed off in itself, but open to the city, to the sea and to the nearest urban fabric. People will always have their heads shaded by leaves, but the space underneath will be very lively and permeable. And if the theme of shade is more and more important today, it is going to become essential to the well-being of city life in the future. The forest will be a true shelter for the city. It is a project that, starting out from a very clear vision on a large scale, then goes into detail on the small one in a painstaking and attentive manner. On our part this has meant a very important and thorough technical study.

How has the forest been designed?

Pierpaolo The approach was to tackle two main aspects in parallel. The first concerned the technical and technological solutions for the planting of the trees, the second concerned the

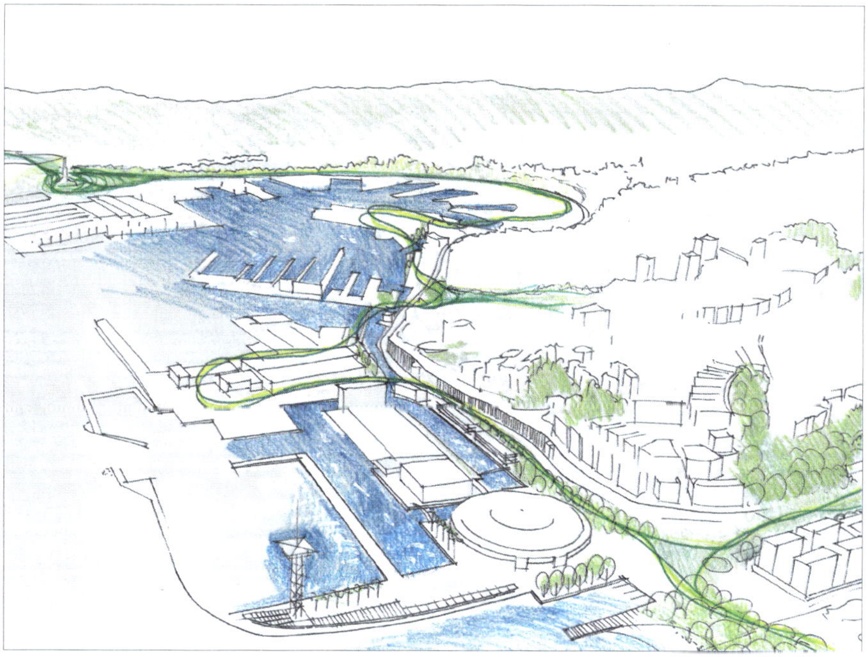

Above: sketch of the overall vision of the system of parks and public areas along the Genoese shoreline. Below: view on the construction site.

On the following pages: aerial view of the project, and view of the forest by the sea that characterise the Waterfront di Levante project.

choice of vegetation. We worked closely with the municipal departments, with which we had an excellent dialogue and an open exchange of views. We started out from a broad range of plants, gradually whittling them down to a smaller and smaller selection with the aim of picking the ones that best answered to all the restrictive environmental parameters of this place, and that would be able to meet the need for sustainability over the long term, with regard both to maintenance – and thus with affordable costs – and vegetation.

So, what are the different figures of landscape that you have used to compose this large forest?

Alessandro The initial idea of the forest was divided up into four kinds of landscape, depending on the specific character of the various parts of the master plan: the first is represented by the gardens of the city walls, a band of Mediterranean maquis that enhances the spaces at the foot of the historical walls and the spaces of access to the area. The second is the row of palm trees, exactly one kilometre in length, that runs along the edge of the area facing the city and the motorway.

Chiara The row of over two hundred palm trees is an iconic element of reference, located between the city and the forest and then the sea, that leads from the promenade of Corso Italia to Batteria Stella, crossing the whole of the new area of the Waterfront. The strong image of the row aims to give a sense of the new system of public spaces, anticipating their presence. In the western part, the tall and slender habit of growth of the palm trees gives a vertical twist to the experience of driving along the elevated motorway, acting as an anticipation of what lies below.

Alessandro The third figure of landscape is the *bosco del mare* or 'forest by the sea', which occupies all the spaces between the row of palm trees, the quays, and the sea.
The appearance of this large space is very urban, and combines the characteristics of the place, the Mediterranean landscape, and the history of Genoa with an allusion to the Spianata dell'Acquasola and other parks in the city. The trees are arranged in a regular grid and the ground is either packed earth or paved in stone, as far as the main routes are concerned; only some parts have an undergrowth of Mediterranean maquis and the use of the space below the foliage is very unconstrained. The fourth figure of landscape is the one on the island surrounded by canals, with the spaces closer to the sea; here the plants chosen are palms again, but of different species, more resistant to the specific atmospheric conditions.

How was the choice of the various plants made?

Pierpaolo The choice of plants was made on the basis of three main requisites: the characteristics of growth of the trees, selected for their form, size, colour and whether they are deciduous or evergreen; the technical one, related to the type of substratum and the depth of soil available in a situation predominantly of roof gardens; and, finally, management and maintenance. So, it was a question of choosing suitable varieties that would be able to combine the structural aspect with the agronomic and management one. In this way we can guarantee on the one hand a certain stability of the project, in both the short and the long term, and on the other maintenance that the municipality will be able to afford and handle. I consider this process to be a truly virtuous one, as we have succeeded in meeting all the requirements and dealing with every aspect of the project, finding the solution best suited to the location.

How do you handle a project as big and complex as the Waterfront?

Paolo The master plan is subdivided into lots, some publicly owned, others private. Based on the preliminary project and the common guidelines we are proceeding with the development of the different areas in a manner consistent with the overall vision.

Georgia One of the main challenges in this sense is the coordination between various disciplines. The experience of the Waterfront has also been of great value in handling the

other assignments we are working on in Genoa, such as the public areas regenerated as a consequence of the project of the tunnel under the harbour, which is of even greater complexity. In processes of regeneration on a large scale like this it is necessary to exercise very close control over the project and tools like BIM, with which we work a lot even though it is still not very developed for the landscaping sector, give us a dynamic interface which can be used to integrate the aspects for which we are responsible with the contributions of the various work groups – of which there are more and more today, one for each sector – from the earliest stages. This allows us to improve coordination and reduce the risks threatening the successful outcome of the project.

Paolo The project for the Waterfront di Levante, along with the ones for the park in Prà and the parks of the tunnel under the harbour, which for us constitute a 'system Genoa', have provided a very important opportunity for research, and above all for a reorganisation of the studies and experiments that AG&P has carried out over the last ten years in relation to green and blue infrastructure in general, and to waterfront projects in particular. Here the intervention of urban regeneration is giving the city's inhabitants back a good and healthy relationship with the sea and with the functions that can be linked with this important element of landscape, through new ways of living in the open able to offer a high quality of life.

MANC
CMCI

Left, below and on the previous page: snapshots of one of the site visit days open to all citizens.

Next page: view of one of the entrances to the Waterfront.

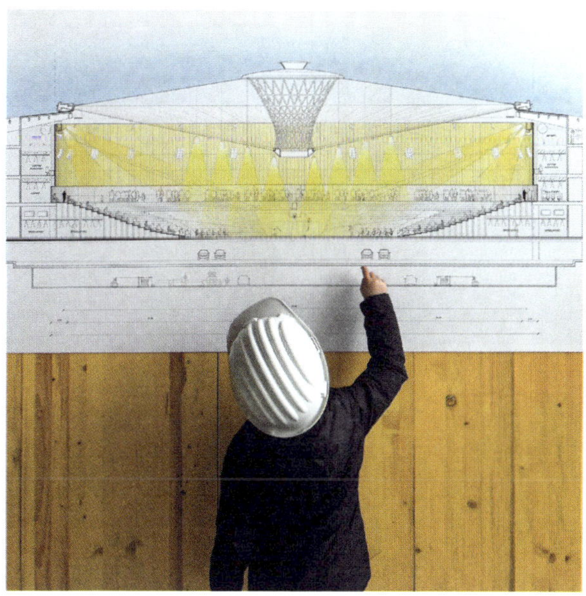

Regenerate to reconnect: the integrated link between public space and landscape

Conversation with

Luigi Priano
partner at RPBW
(Renzo Piano Building Workshop)

Today the city is conceived as a vast organic system made up of constructed space and landscape, one in which nature can and should be playing a connecting role to an ever-greater extent. There is still a certain distance between centre and suburbs, even though, with a view to reducing land take, a process of repossession of the most critical urban areas is underway. RPBW has made regeneration an essential theme of its design. What does it mean to intervene in the built fabric today?

One of the main starting points when tackling a project on any scale is to consider the design of the ground-floor plan as the beginning of each operation, the place in which to stitch together the existing urban fabric and the new intervention. Taking this approach, we like to point out that our projects do not occupy the ground on which they stand but give it back to the city. For over forty years, in fact, the practice has been trying out architectural solutions that set aside large areas for public space, inside or outside the buildings, as an added value in terms of the overall quality of each project. And when it is not possible to find room in the surrounding urban fabric, it becomes necessary to use the ground floors of the buildings, whether new or already existing, for an increasing number of public purposes and functions, making them more permeable, open to flows from the setting in which they are located, with degrees of accessibility that allow people to pass through them as they go about their daily business. We use this approach when drawing up master plans as well, to ensure that we are creating urban fabrics open to the city, that are interconnected and able to generate new synergies and paths of exchange with their context.

Adapting the city in an effective way to the continually changing needs of its inhabitants, but also and above all those of the environment in which we live, for the sake of its conservation, is now a principle which can no longer be disregarded. Themes, these, that you explored in your work years before they became urgent. What role does nature have today in projects of urban regeneration?

Today we are constantly faced with a series of emergencies, that of climate change in the first place. So, when we speak of landscape, it is increasingly necessary to be realistic, to be less alluring and more pragmatic. At whatever scale or in whatever kind of operation we intervene in the city, it is important for landscape to always be an integral part of the project, and not just a decorative element. This is an approach, but also a methodology, in which the studio has a great deal of faith. For example, when we drew up the guidelines of the Waterfront di Levante together with AG&P greenscape, we made it clear to the city council that any garden terracing in the intervention had to have a depth of at least one and a half metres of soil. We insisted on this precisely to favour the presence of a vegetation suited to the location and the project, with a certain size and way of growing, so as to give greater substance and quality to the landscape and the public space of the area as a whole.

We are not always able to make this kind of choice. On some project sites it is not possible to have spaces dedicated to nature. But wherever the opportunity exists, the landscape has to be considered a fundamental element of connection. The Waterfront di Levante is an emblematic intervention in the way that it demonstrates the efficacy of an approach that integrates the landscape into the project. In the initial phases, the decision was taken to build less cubage than was available, turning the areas freed up into a large public park and a small part of this into a navigable canal – taking up the very Genoese theme of the city regaining possession of its sea. The result is a kilometre of landscape facing the sea.

From this perspective, the concept of urban regeneration is also evolving into an approach that perhaps looks beyond the local scale of each intervention.

Today not only it is necessary to integrate the landscape into the project, but it is equally important to look at the boundaries of the intervention to hold a dialogue with spaces all over the city and establish a relationship with them.

We often see localised and circumscribed urban transformations that have little connection with their context, and hardly any at all with the rest of the city. This happens in places that are very different from one another, in the United States, in China, and in Europe too. The need to find immediate solutions to contingent problems, in response to flows of property investments, often leads to an oversimplification of planning processes. In Genoa, on the contrary, we have worked in a synergetic way along the whole coastline. The interventions of the Parco della Lanterna, or AG&P greenscape's Parco delle Dune at Prà, as well as the Waterfront itself, seek to reconnect both the urban fabric and the landscape with the rest of the city.

The former area of the trade fair has always been utilised by the Genoese, even though it was disconnected from the rest of the city. Certainly not an area in which it was easy to intervene.

The former trade fair area is a district the Genoese are very fond of which, widely known, was already a big part of life for those who frequented it when it was still active. For us this was an additional reason to feel an even greater sense of responsibility to realise a project of high quality and accessibility for the city. We often say that the Waterfront project is a sort of synthesis of the characteristics that distinguish the city of Genoa: the area is located on the edge of the port devoted to ship repair; to the north lie the elevated motorway called the Sopraelevata and the historic district of Carignano, much loved by the Genoese; to the south there is the sea, while to the east there is the densely populated district of Foce, filled with notable 19th- and 20th-century buildings. In the space of a linear kilometre, we find all the pieces that make up the identity of this city. The main objective of the project is to reconnect the area with the rest of the urban fabric, fostering the human dimension through pedestrian routes, ample open spaces and a porous ground floor that holds a dialogue with the water and with nature.

What are the main strengths of the Waterfront?

The principal strength has been the decision to free up as much open space as possible, by reducing the volumes of the buildings. In fact, only half the square metres and a third of the cubic metres available in the whole of the area have been built on. There are two important positive aspects to this strategy: on the one hand the clear added value of having public space that is as unencumbered as possible, and on the other the possibility of contributing to the well-being of the environment by turning an extensive area that used to be completely asphalted into a fast-draining surface. A second strength is the design of the spaces on the ground floor, which has favoured that mix of uses, functions and services needed to make the whole of the new district lively and dynamic, with the vitality typical of Italian cities. The third strength is the attention paid to the construction of sustainable buildings, over the medium and long term, using advanced technical and technological solutions. The fourth strong point is undoubtedly the intervention in the existing Palasport building, which has been transformed through an approach of adaptive reuse, in order not to waste the built heritage, seen as an even more valuable resource in view of a future in which it is going to be necessary to construct less and less. A fifth point is the great accessibility of the new district. To achieve such good results, we worked right from the start with the disability manager and pertinent members of Genoa town council and, through a programme of actions, trials and tests of materials and mock-ups of bespoke solutions, we have attained a very high level of integration for the elimination of architectural barriers, something of which we can be proud in the future as well. Finally, it is important to stress the extent to which the new district is connected to the rest of the city through a public transport system that has been extended to this area too. And the landscape is the link that unites the infrastructure systems with the project and integrates them into it.

Public space

The system of open spaces as a landscape resource

Public space, intended as a place offering free access traditionally linked to social, cultural, or economic exchanges between people, has always played a pivotal role in shaping the urban experience across various historical and geographical contexts. The needs and dynamics of today's city are redefining its significance as an essential component of everyday life quality, particularly in densely populated areas.
The 21st century presents an increasingly urgent need to address profound changes in our ecosystem, as well as in social and economic spheres. These changes must be approached with awareness and utilising the resources at our disposal. Global environmental change and associated phenomena, along with the rapid pace of urbanisation, are aspects that must be taken into account as they directly and indirectly impact space, human-made territory, and consequently, the urban landscape.

Currently, urban areas accommodate about 50% of the world's population (and more than 80% of Europe's), residing in small and medium-sized cities, larger towns, metropolitan areas, and mega-cities — a figure expected to exceed by 2050.

In the face of such accelerated and dense urbanisation, with resultant environmental degradation, it becomes evident how public space increasingly embodies not only a protected, safe, and socially recognised meeting place but also a crucial area for the protection, enhancement, and enjoyment of natural resources. If rediscovered or introduced in cities, nature can be a very effective and even less costly tool than other solutions in reducing the impact of climate change and making urban spaces more resilient. Moreover, this strong pressure for growth of built-up areas, as well as its effects in the economy and people's lifestyles, has also brought about major changes in social and cultural behaviours and expectations, which are influencing both the design and maintenance of public spaces. In this new configuration of society and the dynamics of city production, special areas of private ownership and areas subservient to public use often complement and combine with properly public spaces in defining hybrid systems of interconnected open spaces.

This sometimes-controversial phenomenon cannot be overlooked either as an important element in the definition of new urban landscapes or as a factor to be considered in the spatial planning and design of our cities. Nature is a crucial element in the construction of an ecological, symbolic, and utilitarian continuity of these open space systems.

While on the one hand it is important to manage existing public spaces properly in order to guarantee or improve their quality, on the other it is necessary to think very seriously about the need, wherever possible, to plan and design new spaces dedicated to nature and to relate them to each other, in order to reconstruct the ecological and social networks of a new urban landscape, with characters and qualities adapted to the different practices and lifestyles of contemporary society. This project approach also involves experimenting with new forms of public spaces, including inventions, hybridisations and combinations of materials, vegetation, technologies, equipment, imagery, and practices.

A new effective and efficient management of open spaces within the urban fabric must be initiated, studied, and approached with care, if appropriate actions and interventions are to be undertaken to respond to contingent and non-deferrable needs. The years of the recent pandemic have made clear the fragility of public space in our cities, and how much it has been progressively eroded over the last few decades. The need for more open spaces for outdoor activities, with nature nearby, as capillary and interstitial as possible, has emerged loud and clear. In this phase of strong urban development in which the public space is increasingly treated as a product, and not only as part of urban regeneration processes, we need to start designing spaces for people as common goods, in close dialogue with nature.

Identifying and considering the system of public spaces as a landscape resource is a fundamental way to intervene in the built fabric in a strategic, punctual and organic way, looking at nature as an element of rebalancing, a transversal and democratic, social and environmental card to play.

Often parks, gardens and natural spaces in or near our built-up areas serve as symbolic places of escape from the city. It is now necessary to reverse this direction, and to consider nature as an intrinsic presence in the everyday urban experience, in line with a principle of diffused landscape. Consistent with this paradigm shift, a public space planned and managed to meet the development challenges we are facing today can contribute to people's quality of life and social cohesion, as well as redefining our lost sense of place. This aspect is now clear and present in the urban policies of public administration, as well as in the planning of private interventions. The new urban transformation processes, in fact, increasingly require the presence of nature integrated into the project, and very often this involves public open spaces managed by the private developer, or private spaces subjugated to public use, or even landscape interventions of different sizes to compensate for or accompany built projects.

Providing more areas dedicated to the landscape, open to public use, with more functions within them, and an integral part of a natural system that always has to transcend the boundaries of the single intervention, is undoubtedly an opportunity for the development of a quality urban fabric, and for building new spaces for sociality. The challenge requires careful public direction and a precise awareness on the part of all the players involved, starting with the designers.

Adopting this cultural approach to the project, AG&P greenscape has undertaken several projects to redesign urban and public spaces, acting both on the small scale of urban grafting and in the context of wider transformations. The former include the redevelopment of Largo Treves, the creation of the gardens of the residential complex in Via Magolfa, in the Navigli district of Milan, and the Piazza San Francesco in Segrate. The square in Segrate is part of a larger urban landscape system that

Previous page: project view
of the CityWave open space.

Top: the layout of Largo Treves in Milan.

Below, left: view of the gardens open to the public
of the residential complex in Via Magolfa, Navigli
area in Milan.
Below, right: Segrate's pedestrian centre.

Top: view of the pergola in the Cascina Merlata neighbourhood park.
Below: view of the Parco dei Mulini in Segrate.

Below: a view of the skate park in the Parco della Torre in Milan.

redesigns a network of public spaces in the town on the outskirts of Milan as a landscape resource and mitigates the presence of road infrastructure and buildings. These three different places interpret a way of intervening in space, whether public or private put to public use, placing nature at the centre as a tool for reconstructing more balanced relationships between the built fabric and people.

Expanding the scale, the park in the newly developed Cascina Merlata district, located on the outskirts of the city of Milan, and the Parco della Torre are two, albeit different, examples of how today nature and landscape design are at the centre of major urban transformations, and how private initiative facilitates the creation and management of public areas with high quality standards. With reference to the complex dynamics of interrelation between the public and private sectors and the responsibility of being part of large and complex urban property transformation processes, a significant challenge was to integrate and develop a landscape system of the highest environmental quality within a major new development in the CityLife area in Milan: the CityWave project. The construction of what has been conceived by the Copenhagen-based BIG studio (lead designer of the project) as a new gateway to the city, clearly shows how it is possible to integrate nature into the new built environment and how it assumes a breakthrough value in improving the quality of spaces and hospitality for people. Exploiting the virtuous potential of the public-private negotiation experimented by the City of Milan over recent years, the open space project articulates a continuous system of landscapes that integrates parks, squares, paths, and architecture into a single continuous relational fabric in which nature is the protagonist, declined in different ways. This is thanks to specific design, technological and technical solutions that make it possible to bring it even into heavily man-made, urbanised, and artificial contexts such as that of CityLife, with its dense footprint of infrastructure.

Roof gardens represent the most widely used technique for trying to integrate nature into contexts that are often not easy, as in this case. It allows vegetation to be brought to places where it is not possible to have land available, proposing the vision of urban nature as a biological form complementary to the built environment, capable of shaping new architecture, public spaces and adapting to the built heritage.

Roof gardens represent one of the sectors on which AG&P greenscape does the most research and experimentation, with regard also to urban public spaces. Today, it is important to emphasise how the technologies developed in recent years facilitated to bring nature into places that were previously unthinkable and often inaccessible, with a consequent great benefit for not only the environmental aspects, but also those related to people's psychological and physical well-being.

After several completed projects, AG&P greenscape has defined a personal approach to the use of technologies, which need to be contextualised and planned according to the sites of intervention and in dialogue with the architectural project. Because all surfaces dedicated or that can be devoted to nature have the vocation to be part of the diffused landscape, intended as accessible nature and within reach of all people, on which the foundation of the right to nature is based. Trying to go beyond the solutions that already exist on the market, taking time and sometimes assuming risks, the studio attempts to make use of tools and systems that allow pieces of landscape to be created wherever possible. However, it is fundamental that they are already considered at the design stage, sensitising and coordinating the entire interdisciplinary working group, so that nature finds its rightful place from the earliest stages of project conception; and to imagine them as integrated as possible with the context in which they are located, capable of dialoguing also with the surrounding nature. This needs to be done by choosing vegetation that combines aesthetic, ecological and functional qualities, variety, and dynamism, but which can develop adequately and also be durable, reducing risks and maintenance requirements.

The other fundamental aspect when speaking of public space is certainly that of maintenance, intended as an active practice capable of 'feeling' the vegetation, modifying conditions and solutions as needed, following the evolutionary cycles of nature, and assuring its quality and survival over time.

By its very definition, nature is something that changes and evolves with time – which is one of the added values of having it in proximity – and this is precisely why it requires greater attention in planning in the medium and long term, to assure a certain continuity and resistance. The solidity of a new landscape over time can make a significant contribution in socio-ecological terms, providing social, environmental, and aesthetic benefits to its users, both human and non-human. It supports biodiversity and ensures the nourishment of wildlife; it reduces water, soil, and air pollution; it offers spaces for meeting, awareness, and well-being. This is the only way to ensure a sustainable and better future for the urban landscape, for citizens and their quality of life, considered not as a luxury but as a fundamental right. Designing public spaces with a landscape architect's eye therefore does not mean creating an aesthetically pleasing scenography but starting a process for the construction of a place where people and nature meet and grow and evolve together, in the awareness of being part of the same ecosystem, taking care of each other.

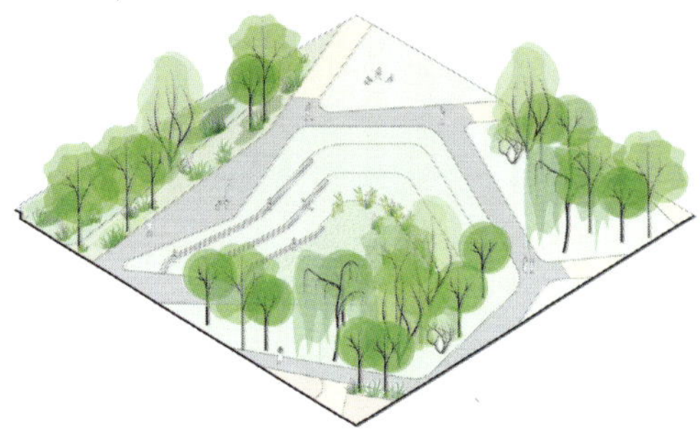

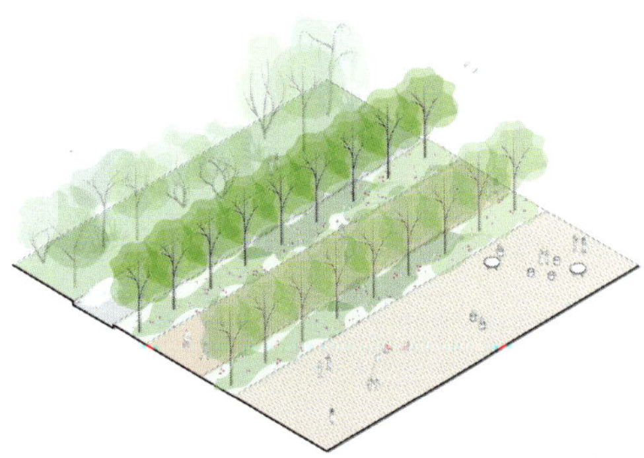

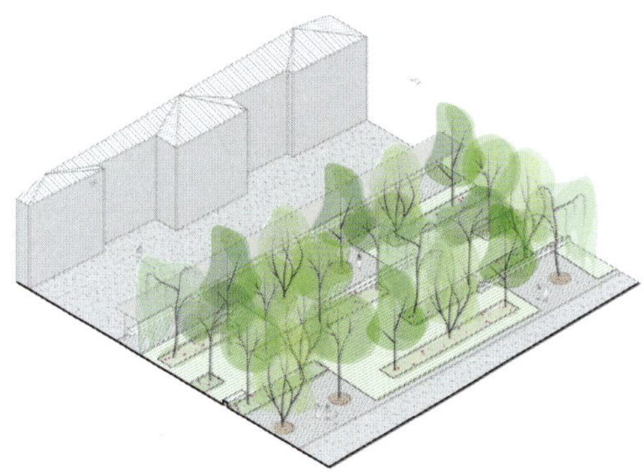

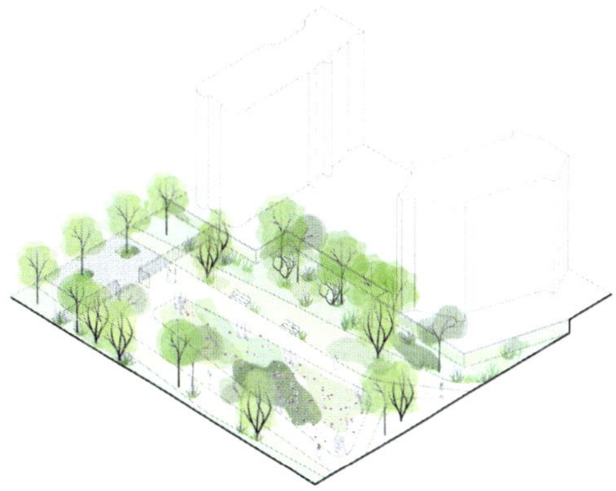

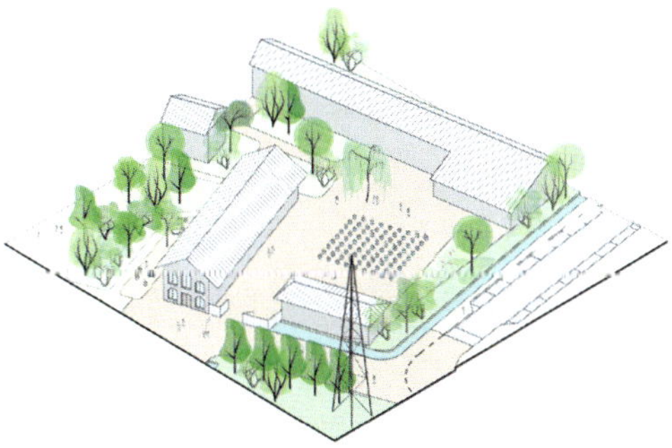

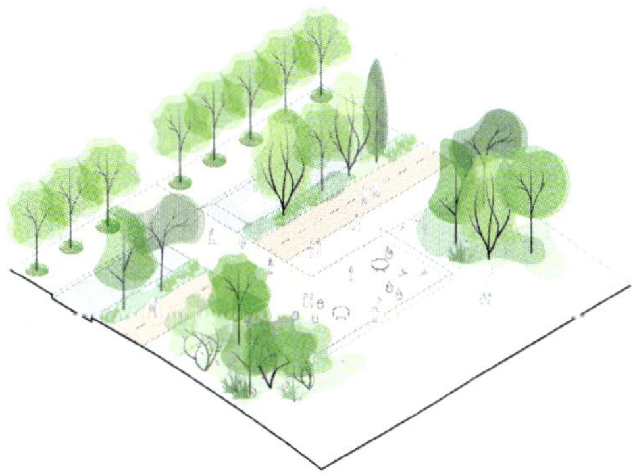

Promenades, commemorative glades, secret gardens, commemorative forests by the sea, water squares, memory gardens, forests of the imagination and others. The selection of axonometric projections exemplifies in a small way the constant design research to integrate the presence of nature in determining places with a socio-ecological value, a challenge that also involves experimenting with new forms of public spaces, including (re)inventions, hybridisations and combinations of materials, vegetation, technologies, equipment, imagery and practices.

New Stadium, Milan

As part of the design studies to imagine the future of the San Siro area, in the proposal elaborated in collaboration with the Manica Group, Sportium Progetto CMR, the park is one of the main tools through which the project fits into the fabric of the surrounding city. With its ten hectares of surface area and almost three thousand tall trees, the area of the new stadium is designed to be one of the tesserae in an already existing urban natural system in the city of Milan.

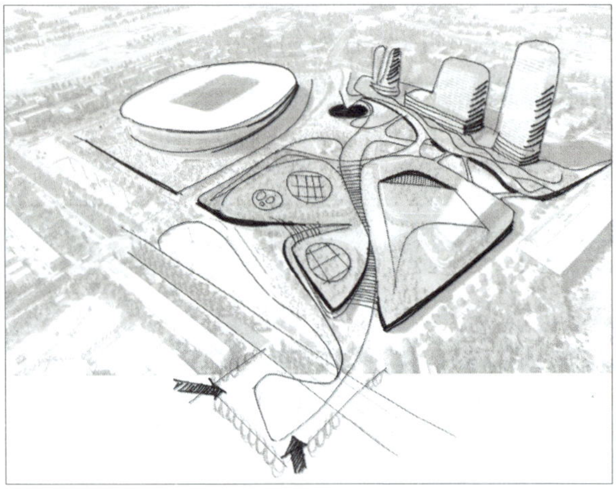

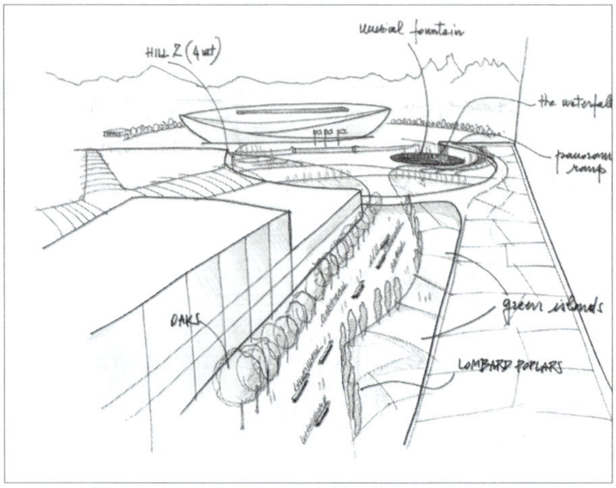

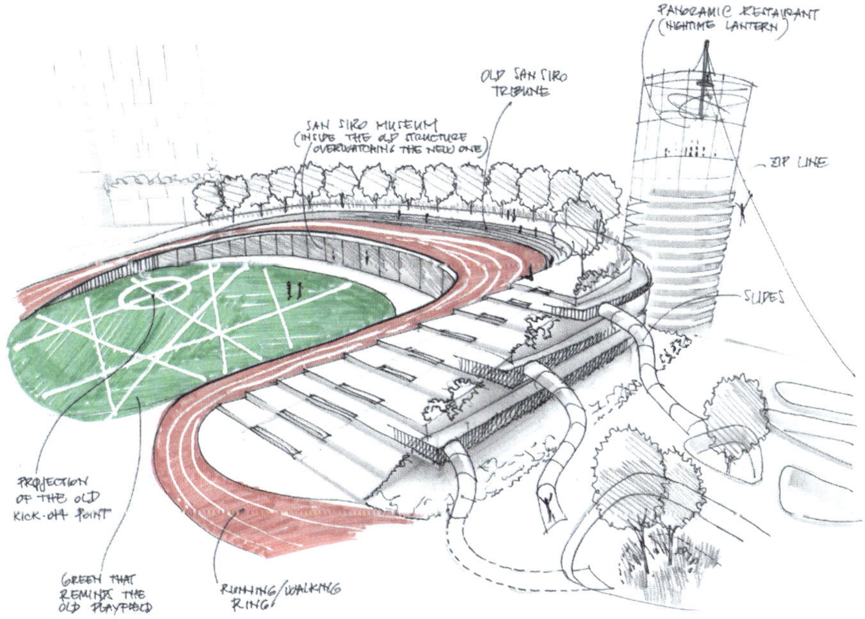
PANORAMIC RESTAURANT
(NIGHTIME LANTERN)
OLD SAN SIRO
TRIBUNE
SAN SIRO MUSEUM
(INSIDE THE OLD STRUCTURE
OVERWATCHING THE NEW ONE)
ZIP LINE
SLIDES
PROJECTION
OF THE OLD
KICK-OFF POINT
GREEN THAT
REMINDS THE
OLD PLAYFIELD
RUNNING/WALKING
RING

SAN SIRO
sports
and
entertainment
park

CityWave, Milan

CityWave is the new complex designed by BIG (Bjarke Ingels Group). It is the last element of the CityLife district in Milan, an ample operation of urban regeneration of the former trade fair area that has been partly open to the public since 2015. CityWave aims to be a new gateway to the district, intended to integrate the area and get it to hold a harmonious dialogue with its context and the rest of the urban fabric. Underneath the great sail that characterises the whole intervention is located the beating heart of the project, a large and new public space conceived as an element of union of the entire complex with the district and designed with the aim of making it a new centre of attraction for the whole city. The concept underpinning the Danish firm's project is that of a building for offices and services in which interior and exterior are continually placed in dialogue. The same design principle has been applied to the landscaping of the intervention, which treats the public space as a large amphitheatre in which nature and architecture communicate, a theatrical backdrop where the daily life of people is put on show to reveal the paths they take. Through the use of solutions and systems of terraced gardens purposely studied and in close dialogue with the architecture, it has been possible to strengthen the presence of nature, both in the public space and in the private courtyards of the complex.

Dialogue with the team

**Emanuele Bortolotti, Paolo Palmulli,
Massimo Brignoli, Giorgia Fiorentini,
Barbara Frangi, Irene Grieco,
Michele Pasculli, Pierpaolo Tagliola**

The CityWave project explores several important aspects of public space: on the one hand, the virtuous relationship between the private and public sector to realise quality open spaces, and on the other hand the ability, through tailor-made solutions, to bring nature into less easy contexts.

Paolo Major urban transformations are now an important opportunity to create innovative and high-quality open spaces. The presence of nature plays a fundamental role in balancing the impact of these transformations and proposing urban models for the city of the future that have nature as a determining and positive element for people and the planet.
If we look at the processes to achieve this result, the added value of the virtuous relationship between the public and private sectors can be found in several aspects: the high quality of open spaces, which can be designed and implemented at costs often not accessible to the public sector; their maintenance, a fundamental aspect when we talk about open spaces; and, finally, the possibility of creating more surfaces dedicated to nature, contributing to improving the quality of the widespread landscape as a great element of value.

CityWave, in fact, was just the first project in the area. You went on to do more.

Barbara The project we did for CityWave has provided the opportunity to reflect on and intervene in other areas of CityLife, bringing vegetation into different contexts. To make sure that each intervention is harmonious, we have looked at the whole area as a single body, insisting considerably on continuity with the type of elements that were already there, whether vegetation, street furniture or finishing materials. Looking at the existing park as a reference for more specific interventions too has allowed us to choose those species of plants that had already shown to be well-suited to the environment, using the experience to our advantage.

What principles did you apply when designing CityWave's open space?

Massimo In following the development of open spaces, the main objective has always been to make the landscape project of CityWave coherent with the park and green areas of CityLife, to generate a continuous public space where a certain permeability of sight and sense is guaranteed between the outside and the inside, in the various gradients of use, from private to privately served to public, to public. The design of the open space, from the choice of vegetation and finishing materials, such as pavements, to tailor-made technological solutions, has been designed precisely to create this sense of continuity.

In a complex project like CityLife, where a series of different interventions have followed one another over time, having an approach to its realisation that holds a dialogue with the context to ensure a greater continuity between the different routes and areas, is undoubtedly an added value.

TAXI TAXI
B
A

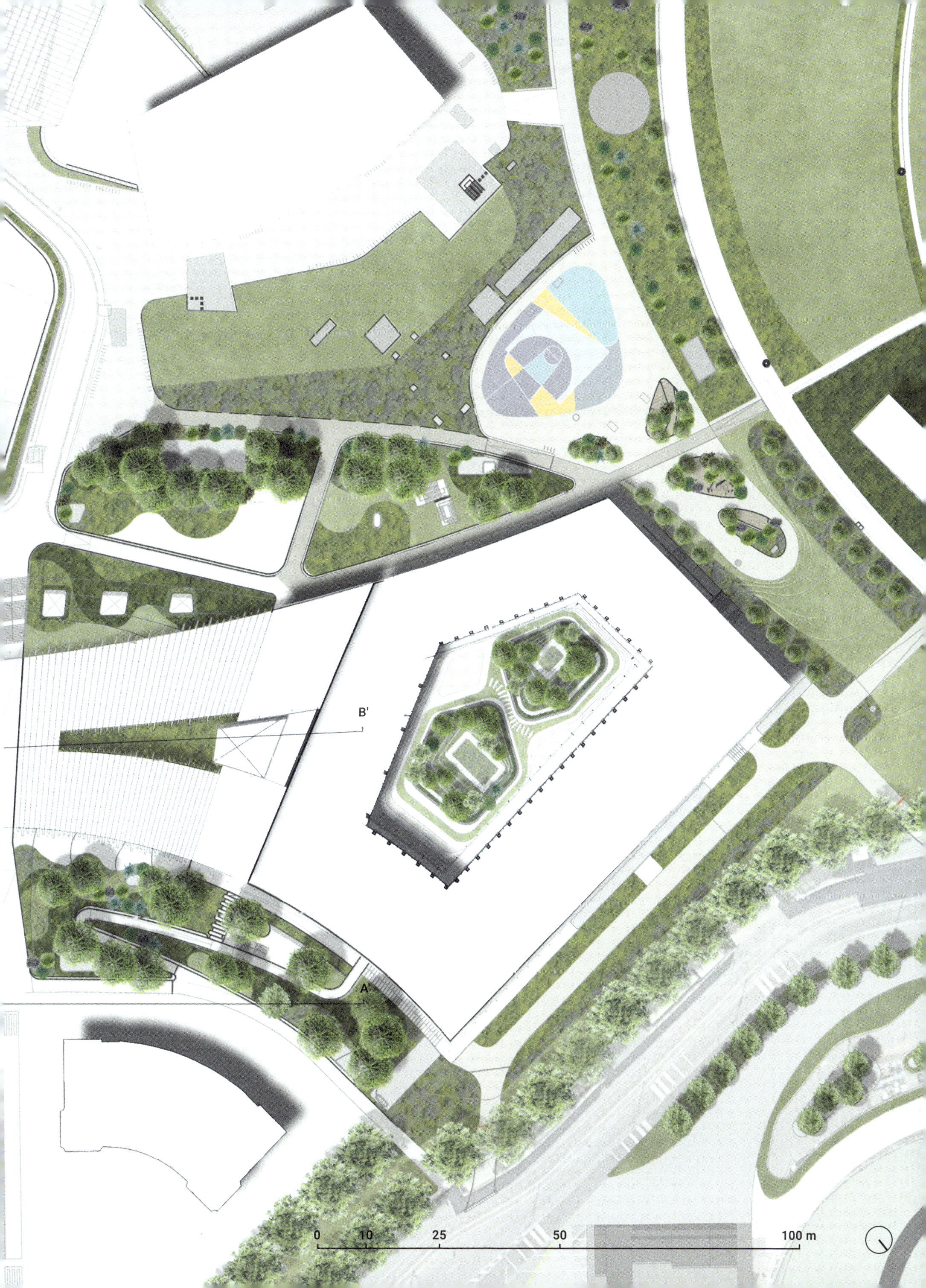
B'
A'
0
10
25
50
100 m

On the previous page: plan of the CityWave open space.

On these pages: two longitudinal sections of the CityWave open space.

On the following pages: a view of the area of the future entrance to the CityWave complex, two project views, and a view of the site area.

A–A'

B–B'

Paolo A continuity that seeks above all the diffused quality of the design, which is the main aspect, but also the most important and ultimate objective. It is necessary for the new public spaces of the city, especially in areas as large as CityLife, to be comfortable for the people who are going to live there, who are going to pass through them on a daily basis and in a ritual of new routes that is yet to be established. Today the quality of public spaces is increasingly indispensable to the success of an intervention of transformation or regeneration of an area. Being able to bring nature into these projects, even where it is not obvious that there is any room for it, is an added value of urban landscape design in which we believe strongly.

Emanuele The design of the stairs in the central space of the project, protected by the canopy, goes precisely in that direction, to offer an open and comfortable public space in which to stop and pause. And in that pause comes into play the scenography and choreography of the lives of people who pass through or use that covered space, designed as a sort of contemporary amphitheatre, in a variety of ways.

Projects developed by foreign studios often have to be adapted to some extent to comply with current Italian regulations, which we know to be much less permissive than elsewhere in Europe. How have you dealt with this aspect?

Irene The dialogue with BIG has been continuous and open. In the section for which we are responsible, we have tried to find constructive solutions to the problems that have arisen. Solutions that have been refined to the point where they were made an integral part of the project from the start.

Massimo The zig-zag walkway that spans the two central flights of steps, for instance, was a solution that had to be adapted to comply with the regulations. Although not easy to realise, it is interesting precisely because it proposes a different way of utilising the almost canonical space for our latitudes of an urban flight of steps that recalls the geometry of an amphitheatre.

Giorgia It shows how important the figure of the so-called local architect is in managing the construction process of an international project and the delicate and complex mediation between the property's needs, the municipality's regulations, and the foreign designer's design choices. Increasingly, it is no longer just a question of playing the role of mediator but also a technical-artistic one, sharing design solutions and a landscape vision.

Milan has to some extent rediscovered the value and potential of public space thanks to the numerous recent projects that have changed the connotations of the city; projects such as CityLife but also Porta Nuova, which also includes the Biblioteca degli Alberi Milano. How can nature best be integrated into these urban transformation processes based on the enhancement of public space?

Massimo In CityWave the vegetation represents a sort of second skin of an organism that is wholly artificial but capable of producing landscape on a par with any other more traditional type of open space, thanks to the technologies of terraced gardens and green roofs. Taking nature where it is needed and creating the conditions for its presence requires a very high level of technological and technical expertise. Moveover, following talks with the project team, inside and outside the studio, we reached a point where the design of the open space for CityWave became an outline to which the structural project has adapted as well, this is an aspect of considerable importance, given that we are accustomed to treating the landscape as the final stage in the realisation of a project.

For CityWave as for other projects, from Bosconavigli to Monte Rosa 91, as well as some residential schemes, the studio has always come up with bespoke technical solutions for the terraced and roof gardens.

One of your characteristics is a wide-ranging vision of how nature can be brought into all urban settings, even the most difficult, together with the intense experimentation that lies behind each of these operations.

Pierpaolo Increasingly today, we have to be able to find suitable ways to accommodate the natural landscape in our cities ensuring it thrives, through an understanding of the context where we are working each time, finding the right proposals. And above all, we have to be aware that aiming for a sustainable future signifies not just planting trees, but also ensuring that they are able to live as long as possible. Today, green terrace and roof technologies and techniques allow us to explore new solutions, greatly increasing the possibility of having more areas of vegetation in the city, with all the benefits that come from it.

Emanuele *Il giardino inaspettato* (The Unexpected Garden), one of the books I have written drawing on the experience and know-how gained in the studio over time, is a move towards that precise direction. Through research, experimentation and refinement of some of the types of green terrace and roof that already exist, we can really think about having a diffused landscape all over the city. We often hear people saying that we ought to be planting trees and introducing vegetation everywhere. This can be done, but only with ever more technologically advanced approaches and solutions that allow the operation to be sustainable, from every point of view.

Michele Acting according to these principles requires the best balance between more natural and more technological solutions, to manage the evolution of the new project ecosystems sustainably, while at the same time seeking the greatest well-being for users, both human and non-human. In CityWave, for example, the presence of vegetation favours and improves the quality of the open space, both in environmental terms and in terms of liveability and aesthetics. This combination not only contributes to important microclimatic aspects, but also to people's psychological and physical well-being in general. This is why the search for the best solutions for hanging gardens, combined with the selection of plants, has been important in imagining a quality contemporary public space.

In fact, roof and terrace garden systems are now part of the nature-based solutions and fall within the series of minimal environmental criteria needed to achieve heat reduction in urban centres. What were the biggest challenges you faced?

Pierpaolo At CityWave we have had to manage the weight of the roof and terrace gardens, which rested on enormous volumes located partly or completely below ground level. For this reason, we had to work on specific solutions to fill the gaps and give the plants the right depth of soil, without placing too heavy a burden on the spaces beneath. It was a question of developing a system of great equilibrium between the different technological and natural parts, coming up with customised solutions and holding a dialogue with the context and the architectural design.

Emanuele Today, the use of hanging gardens brings considerable advantages, from reduction of temperatures in urban areas to the reduction of air pollutants, to the increase of water catchment areas, reducing the presence of impermeable ones, and the consequent increase of the resilience of urban systems in cases of periods of great need or intense rainfall. In addition, these technologies allow us to bring vegetation to places that are often unthinkable or inaccessible, with a consequent great benefit that concerns environmental aspects, in the first instance, but also those related to the psychological and physical well-being of people.

The role of public space in major urban transformations

Conversation with

Paolo Micucci CEO of CityLife
Roberto Russo CEO of SmartCityLife

The role of public space has become ever more central to the success of schemes of urban regeneration on a large scale, from both the functional and practical viewpoint and the financial one. How have you seen this change in recent years?

Paolo Micucci: The CityWave project was drawn up by one of the most visionary and innovative architects of our time – Bjarke Ingels – someone who is attentive to the evolution in the way spaces are used precisely in relation to the public space in which it is inserted. In fact CityWave will create a large new covered plaza, perfectly integrated into the setting of the public park that is already one of the main green lungs of the city of Milan today, and of the office spaces that will occupy the East and West buildings, sustainable and highly efficient from the viewpoint of their energy use. The new project will also redesign the road system of the CityLife district, acting as the entrance from the north-east and thus an additional point of dialogue with the rest of the city as well as the three existing towers, always placing the emphasis on sustainable mobility and pedestrian traffic. It was precisely these aspects of integration and interpenetration of public and private space, of inside and outside, of vegetation and the built, of the covered plaza and the open-air park, that won us over right from the competition phase. In fact we were looking for a project not just of the highest architectural quality that would be able to 'complete without competing', but that also answered to the new requirements for the utilisation of spaces, both indoors and out.

In what way does the CityWave project answer to the new needs of contemporary public space?

Paolo Micucci: CityWave will face onto an open area that is not a mere park, but the beating heart of CityLife's smart city, replete with services and usable by the public in full security. During the period of the pandemic, we were able to see just how crucial urban green spaces are for the quality of life, and all over Europe the demand remains high for buildings with elevated standards, not just from the viewpoint of the environment, but increasingly from that of social life and governance as well.

Was the realisation of a large public park as the beating heart of the entire project in CityLife's intentions from the start?

Roberto Russo: CityLife's public park is a vital and central space for the whole project of urban regeneration of the former Milan trade fair area. To maximise the environmental and operating potentialities of this park, which is the second largest area of greenery in the city centre, we already paid the maximum of attention in the planning phase (outcome of an international competition staged and coordinated with the public administration) to the choice of plants and the relations and dimensions of the usable spaces. In fact, the park will have a vast open area to be used for events, trees of different sizes that will provide shaded areas, various lawns with gentle slopes where people can lie down and relax, paved squares where to meet up in and paths that change their dimensions and type of paving in relation to the hierarchy. To make the park even better and livelier, we have also set up Smart-CityLife, which has three main objectives: environmental quality, security and accessibility. In our view, being smart doesn't just mean using technology – even though we have created a special app to make everything simpler and bring it within everyone's reach – but above all paying attention to the requirements of the almost 11 million people who pass through and use the park every year.

The contemporary public park, especially if inserted in newly laid-out districts, is often accompanied by a plan of extraordinary activities. What programmes have you launched to bring it to life?

Roberto Russo: The main programmes are linked to sports, cultural and social activities. Introducing a magnificent Padel Pavilion with nine padel courts and a sports centre with four tennis courts, as well as running events, CityLife is establishing itself as one of the places of reference for all Milanese marathons. From the cultural viewpoint, one of our showpieces is ArtLine, an open-air museum with over 20 permanent site-specific sculptures created by young artists of international reputation, while the spaces of the park lend themselves to music events open to all.

From a social perspective, the park is an extraordinary gathering place thanks to events on a small and large scale, even those of more national significance, such as the passage of the historic Mille Miglia road race, an occasion for an unforgettable day out in a unique setting.

In short, an ambitious and multifaceted programme of management that has required a substantial work of preparation with all the complexities that can be imagined, but with enormous positive repercussions on the entire district in the coming years.

In terms of environmental sustainability and biodiversity, the presence of nature in our city is becoming ever more fundamental, from a perspective of 'diffused landscape', in which every area of vegetation helps to improve the quality of our urban spaces. What 'green strategies' have you brought into the CityLife area as well as into its immediate surroundings?

Paolo Micucci: CityLife's public park currently covers 17 hectares and has over 2,000 trees, including maples, oaks, chestnuts, and limes, and will be further expanded with the realisation of CityWave. In the design of the park, great attention was paid to the choice of varieties, to alternate zones of more lush vegetation with other more open areas of grass, boosting local biodiversity by encouraging the spontaneous germination of flora and the arrival of 'urban' fauna, such as squirrels, rabbits and numerous species of pollinating insects and birds. Also located in the park, the Orti Fioriti, an area of over 5,000 sqm laid out in collaboration with the Associazione Orticola di Lombardia with gardens of aromatic and medicinal herbs, flowers, and locally sourced vegetables.

The unique characteristic of CityLife's park is the perfect integration of its green landscape with urban elements, such as the buildings designed by world-famous starchitects, the contemporary artworks of ArtLine, the sports facilities devoted to tennis and padel, the areas equipped for fitness or for children, the highly sustainable BabyLife playschool with its unique design aimed at meeting the needs of the youngest and helping them discover nature. Not only vegetation, but water too plays a leading role in the park, with the drinking trough of ovoid shape fed by a system of recirculation so as not to waste the precious resource and the historic Fontana delle Quattro Stagioni, a fountain dating from 1927 that has been perfectly restored and integrated into the context. And so CityLife's park takes shape as a green, public, urban, and smart space, where nature enters the city, improving the quality of life.

Dwelling

Living in contact with nature

Following the Covid-19 pandemic, there has been a realisation of how much visual and physical contact with nature is an increasingly fundamental aspect both for the well-being of people living in urban centres and for the city itself. Countless studies over the last few decades have, with data and numbers in hand, demonstrated how nature plays a major role in improving living conditions in urban environments; not only is its influence in regulating those important environmental processes that assure the reproduction of the resources necessary for the survival of all living species increasingly evident, but it also clearly conditions various aspects of people's psycho-physical well-being.

In the urban context, nature, understood as a system, and as often emphasised in other parts of this book, produces important effects for the protection of the environment: it lowers particulate matter in the air, attenuates noise, counteracts rising temperatures, increases soil quality, and ensures that the city is connected to natural rhythms and the presence of various animal and plant species. The ecosystem services that natural systems generate, whether they are material (support, regulation, supply) or immaterial (cultural), have a significant impact on the quality of life in urban centres that must always be considered in all phases of intervention on the built environment, and at all scales too. And for natural ecosystems to be able to support these services, it is necessary for ecological processes to continue to be preserved, in such quantity and quality to assure that their functionality is not compromised.

For these reasons, and in this urban condition, even the transformation or construction of new housing represents an important opportunity to preserve the role of nature and related ecosystem. The progressive densification of major urban centres contributes to the urgency of the need to think about residential architecture in a more integrated way between the urban fabric and nature, combining planning, design, management, and care of the built and natural environment.

Today, landscape design plays a fundamental role in influencing the present and especially the future of our cities, considering 'sustainable living' in a way that is always integrated and inclusive, from an economic, environmental, and social point of view.

A private garden pertaining to one or more residential buildings can have the same value as an urban park for the city: its presence alone determines and brings all those positive aspects in improving the quality of life not only of people, but also of nature itself, in terms of safeguarding and supporting biodiversity. In the concept of 'diffused landscape', which the studio has been pursuing for some time, each area dedicated to nature becomes part of a landscape system, of which each natural element is a piece, capable of working in synergy and in a network, even on a city-wide scale.

The task of the landscape designer, in this particular area, is to experiment with ideas and interventions capable of offering different solutions, where aesthetics and functionality work together simultaneously to preserve the systemic ecological benefits and to bring out the beauty of nature within the urban space as an added value.

The social value of urban nature has the capacity to make our lives healthier, improve everyday conditions, and provide spaces for socialisation and well-being. In order to achieve these benefits, it is increasingly important to design spaces dedicated to nature, even if only small ones – large areas are not necessary –, for, if well designed, residential areas lend themselves perfectly to becoming pieces of a larger, integrated nature system.

The key words are quality and intensity. Allowing a fluid and continuous transition between private, semi-public, and public areas in a system capable of generating continuous exchanges and connections is a strategic way of integrating spaces dedicated to nature into a broader landscape vision.

Starting from these considerations, and from the concept of landscape as a system of diffuse nature, the studio has completed some important projects in the residential sector. From interventions on common condominium spaces to the more integrated master plans for the development of entire residential areas, vegetation is the instrument through which new ways of living in contact with nature are experienced. In the case of the residential complex in Bergamo or the Opificio in Via Magolfa in Milan, nature plays a tidying role in the various open and pertinent areas, but also an aesthetic and environmental one, with a variety of plants and flowers suited to their surroundings. While, in the residential building in Via Garibaldi in Milan, the vegetation of the terraces on all floors of the building is treated as a scenic backdrop, changing colour with the passing of the seasons, capable of communicating with the scale of the city, but also with that of the private home.

The Giardino delle Scoperte in Segrate, on the other hand, is a larger project, the result of the design of a master plan for a residential area, where the system of open spaces has been conceived as a continuous landscape resource. Within it there are paths, small gardens, thematic spaces, combined in a unified landscape system designed with all possible users in mind, from children to young people, to the elderly, and to reveal its qualities with the rhythm of the seasons.

All the activities have been calibrated so that summer, autumn, spring and winter, as well as evening and morning, have a place to express their vitality. It constitutes an important addition to the large surrounding park, Centroparco.

However, the most experimental residential projects were Bosconavigli in Milan and the Merezzate Smart District in the Rogoredo area

On the previous page:
a view of the inner garden
of Bosconavigli in Milan.

Top: the Discovery Garden,
part of the residential complex
Centroparco Life in Segrate.
Below: the open space of Residenze
Bergamo+.

On the next page, top: the courtyard of the
Opificio residential complex in Via Magolfa,
Milan; below: view of the Habitaria residential
building in Corso Garibaldi 95 in Milan.

of Milan. In both cases, nature was conceived as an integrated tool of well-being and dialogue with people and the surrounding urban fabric.

Bosconavigli in Milan, designed with the studios Stefano Boeri Architetti and Arassociati, investigates and experiments with vegetation that becomes landscape from the architecture to the urban scale. Nature, distributed on the terraces on each floor, is seen as the second skin of an artificial organism, capable of mediating and restoring a sense of balance between the vegetation, the city, the building and the people who will inhabit it. On the urban scale, an integrated and cohesive system of vegetation starts from the building and, through the pathways and condominium areas, intercepts the linear park arranged along the Naviglio Grande, which reconnects with the road network and the spaces dedicated to nature in the neighbourhood and the entire city.

The Merezzate social housing project, on the other hand, was an interesting opportunity for AG&P greenscape, responsible for the landscape design of the open spaces, to question the relationship between social housing and landscape design.

A fundamental aspect was the synergy between urban, landscape and architectural design to offer quality open spaces that could become active and supervised places for building and developing the community of residents, a crucial aspect for a new neighbourhood located in an area that still has few urban features in its surroundings.

The landscape design of the open spaces, drawn up in close synergy with the master plan concept, builds a system of relations that defines the gradient between public, semi-public and private space, integrating built and natural areas, areas equipped for sports and play, gardens, paths and squares, trees, mown and flowered lawns, and community gardens. Along the central axis, in the various neighbourhood courtyards and in the garden courts, the project envisages a rich presence of nature so that it is always part of the daily experience of all inhabitants, both when walking in or out of the spaces (the whole neighbourhood is pedestrianised), and when looking out of the windows of their flats or while using the community or neighbourhood's commercial services. Working in an integrated way right from the concept of the neighbourhood master plan was essential to contain costs and at the same time offer a high-quality result. With this same focus on economic sustainability, the project envisaged choices that would allow for sustainable management methods and costs over time, with results that are already tangible on a daily basis in the life of the neighbourhood.

A diverse urban nature is not only essential for the quality of ecosystem services, climate adaptation and support of a socially well-functioning city; biodiversity also acts as the basis for our mental and physical health and well-being.

Stressing an *ecocentric* view of the world is crucial if we are to integrate all the benefits that nature can bring to our cities. We must collaborate with nature when we tackle urban development and start designing our cities, not just for the sake of humanity, but for life, all lives.

Merezzate Smart District, Milan

The new Merezzate neighbourhood lab project was born from the virtuous synergy between the City of Milan and Redo. Under the banner of sustainable living, the project explores the relationship between social housing and landscape design. Built based on a close synergy between urban, landscape, and architectural intervention, the public spaces project was conceived as a generator of new urban dynamics, defining a gradient between public, semi-public, and private space. The aim is to promote sociality and support collaborative and sustainable living, while at the same time ensuring that nature is always part of the daily experience of all the inhabitants.

1.

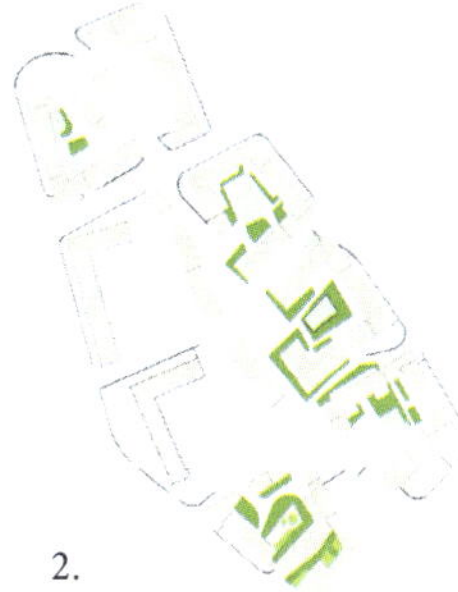

2.

3.

1. Trees and vegetation
2. Neighbourhood courts
3. Playgrounds

On the next page: view from above of Bosconavigli.

Bosconavigli, Milan

Bosconavigli is a residential development intervention by the Stefano Boeri Architetti and Arassociati practices, with landscape design by AG&P greenscape. Promoted by Milanese private operators, the new housing complex will be at the centre of a profound redevelopment of the area, which will connect the zone of Tortona with that of the Navigli, regenerating Via San Cristoforo. Through the creation of foot and cycle paths, areas of landscaping and open spaces with services and facilities, the project will represent an important step towards the reforestation of that urban setting, in which the presence of nature is only marginal.

Bosconavigli is conceived, therefore, as a living and sustainable organism. Its vegetation system is intended to filter particulate matter and lower pollution, while reducing energy consumption through the thermal inertia of its plants, which provide protection from the rays of the sun and absorb CO_2. The great variety of shrubs and other kinds of vegetation that outline and cover the façades of the Bosconavigli have a twofold value: on one hand they create the environment best suited to favouring biodiversity, and on the other they will modify the colours and profiles of the building with the change in seasons.

Dialogue with the team

Emanuele Bortolotti, Paolo Palmulli, Paolo Maneo, Mariagiusi Troisi, Stefania Zavarise

Bosconavigli is located at a particularly significant point in the urban fabric, by the canal called Naviglio Grande.

Paolo M. Yes, the area where the project is located is definitely an interesting one, on both the urban and the architectural scale. Bosconavigli is part of a more general strategy of reuse of abandoned areas, optimisation of open areas and improvement of public spaces, overcoming the infrastructural barriers between districts. In fact, the project is located at a pivotal point, as it were, that opens and connects the dense and stratified fabric of the city with one of its historical districts, where a series of transformations have been carried out along the Naviglio Grande, starting from the station of Porta Genova, moving south to the station of San Cristoforo.

Emanuele Nature is the main protagonist of Bosconavigli, on the urban scale as well as that of the building. The project is set in an area with 3,550 sqm of private and over 7,000 sqm of public park. It is an important green lung, in a part of the city where nature is very thin on the ground, and this cannot help but be a great opportunity of renewal for the whole district, in the spirit of sustainability and biodiversity.

Moreover, the project clearly shows how important it is to plan each intervention in the built environment with a strategy that looks at and integrates with its context, to favour a more programmatic diffused landscape.

Generally, had it already been envisioned as an intervention especially surrounded by greenery?

Mariagiusi Yes, the project is to all intents and purposes part of a larger urban project of open spaces dedicated to nature and public paths along the Naviglio Grande. The aim was to redesign the approach to the promenade on the water, but also to connect better the consolidated part of the city and the area of the church of San Cristoforo with a cycle-pedestrian path, enhancing what is a small yet special place in the city. At the moment, the project envisages a path immersed in the landscape, which, once the railway tracks will have been removed, will find space to continue towards the area to the south-west. The main idea, based on which the paths and landscape areas have been designed, is to leave traces so that the open space project can grow in the future.

How was the Bosconavigli project born?

Paolo The project began with the ambition of transforming a space of poor urban quality, partly used as a landfill site, into a special place where nature had the ability to mend the urban fabric and offer a high quality of life. And the challenge had a long gestation.

Mariagiusi It was almost finished, until in the working group with Stefano Boeri and Arassociati, after the pandemic, it was decided to revise it completely, rethinking the value of open space and the presence of nature as even more fundamental aspects to be considered, increasing private green spaces for residents, but also thinking of facilitating collective activities in the communal and outdoor areas.

0
5
10
15
25
50 m

Have there also been structural changes to the building?

Mariagiusi Yes, again in the general overhaul phase of the project it was decided to make the terraces and balconies larger, as well as the spaces for bikes, leaving more room for vegetation and people, with the aim of facilitating collective activities in the common areas and the open air. This allowed us to propose a project of broader scope, with a lot of services and a greater amount of open space, both in the building's common areas and in the individual housing units.

A vegetation that on the urban scale holds a harmonious dialogue with the plants present on the façades of the building, studied to suit the needs of each of them.

Emanuele That's right. An aspect on which we did a lot of work was the selection of the vegetation on the façades. The local climate situation is changing very rapidly, so we had to think about the need to choose plants and trees that would be able to resist for a longer time, to make the project more sustainable with the passing of the years.

The presence of vegetation on the façade has often prompted great concern on the part of public opinion on the question of its management and maintenance. How is maintenance carried out at Bosconavigli?

Mariagiusi Thinking about these more practical and everyday aspects, we have designed the landscape to make maintenance more simple and accessible, in terms of cost too. In fact, the external façades only are green, so that the work of maintenance can be done from the outside. For the internal façades, we have envisaged each of the housing units being able to handle maintenance on its own, finding suitable solutions for the installations.

Bosconavigli presents us, in fact, with a highly technological type of nature. It is because of the detailed study of innovative solutions that we can now have greenery in places where it has not always been possible to have it. Other examples of this kind are CityWave and the Pocket Campus.

Mariagiusi Yes, nature is present in Bosconavigli thanks to technological solutions developed for the purpose. For each terrace we have worked on different aspects, from the method of providing a substrate to the systems of anchorage and irrigation. We have come up with a better package of substrate for the tubs containing the plants, making it possible for them to grow even in a small space, with each plant anchored to its own terrace. In addition, we have taken steps to ensure that the irrigation system can run as autonomously as possible. And it is thanks to these technological solutions that Bosconavigli's rich and varied vegetation has an environmental value, and not just a decorative one.

Stefania We have often found ourselves working in complex situations in other residential projects as well, even if not experimental ones like Bosconavigli. In some we had very low depths of soil available, few loads, containers that were too small or overly narrow. In such cases, it is necessary to have enough experience to find suitable solutions that can bring nature into difficult settings as well and ensure that the plants will be able to survive and grow. The awareness of the value of the presence of greenery in residential projects as well has now greatly increased. It is to be hoped that in the future this will lead to a more integrated, if not obligatory, use of vegetation in all projects.

Paolo This is why it is important to raise the awareness of all those involved in the design process to integrate landscape design skills already at the very early stages of building design, to minimise issue and maximise the quality of the result, as in Bosconavigli.

Returning to Bosconavigli, how have the plants used on the façades been chosen?

Mariagiusi Great attention has been paid to the generation of an environment that is as natural, varied, and biodiverse as possible, considering the setting in which the building is located, the Navigli, with the waterway close by.

Previous pages: plan and aerial view
of the Bosconavigli residential complex.

On this page: three main elevations
of the residential complex.

On the next page: evening view
of the complex's inner courtyard.

We have taken various themes into consideration, from ecology to biodiversity, trying to create a natural environment where it would be pleasant to live surrounded by greenery both indoors and outdoors, that would give people a sense of well-being when looking at it not only from the outside, but from the inside too. This is why we have devoted the same care to every single balcony and terrace, designing many different types of planters to suit what is going to grow in them and setting about the design of the façades as if it were a jigsaw puzzle. The idea was to have a certain variety of plants for each floor, balcony, and terrace, but also uniform patches of vegetation on the façades.

All this seems easy enough to say but is very complex to accomplish.

Mariagiusi Yes, it has been very complicated, because for each floor we have had to take account of both the adjoining content and the overall design. So, we have worked with the colours, heights, and habit of growth of the trees, always seeking to create a harmonious, wholly bespoke appearance for each façade, combined with ecological richness.

Could urban interventions like Bosconavigli be seen as a pioneering example?

Emanuele In general, something has changed in the approach to choosing the vegetation for projects, be they public or private, on the urban or architectural scale. However, further steps need to be taken. Projects like Bosconavigli ought to be opportunities to tackle this theme and try to diversify urban landscapes, testing the efficacy of solutions that go beyond the rhetoric of greening at any cost and really take ecosystemic aspects into consideration.

Stefania The solutions that we are presenting are designed above all to make the projects sustainable in the long run. When dealing with a living organism like vegetation, which changes with the seasons, thinking about a project for the long term is fundamental. We are already seeing excellent results, and, in a few years, we will have an even more complete picture of the results and potential of the experiments we are conducting today.

The spaces of contemporary dwelling: a green revolution in the dialogue between nature, city and architecture

Conversation with

Stefano Boeri
Stefano Boeri Architetti

Bosconavigli is a housing complex designed in the spirit of a more advanced, broadened concept of sustainability, one that comprises nature as an element essential to the protection and quality of the environment, to the well-being not just of people, but of other species too. What are the innovative aspects of this project?

Bosconavigli, under construction since October 2022, is a green work of architecture that adapts the model of the Bosco Verticale to a building of low density in the neighbourhood of San Cristoforo, a point of junction between the city and the area of the Ticino River and the Alzaia del Naviglio in Porta Ticinese.

At the architectural level, the main innovation of the design is its reworking of the type of the courtyard house, characteristic of the Lombard tradition: the volume has a spiral arrangement that makes it possible to exploit the progressive variation in heights (up to a maximum of 11 levels) to create green terracing with the aim of favouring and maximising the use of open spaces, both public and private, and the relationship with the surrounding natural context – the steps of the building descend progressively towards the Parco Sud, preparing for a future single green connection with the project of the railway yard.

The presence and integration of vegetation is, in and of itself, a fundamental aspect of the intervention: Bosconavigli is in fact characterised by the presence of 170 trees, from 60 different species, together with shrubs and climbing plants, located on the façades, roofs, terraced gardens and balconies. Elements that form a natural screen and help to absorb CO_2 and particulate matter, shading the internal spaces and making the place more liveable for its occupants.

Where energy is concerned as well, solutions have been adopted to make the building more sustainable.

Yes, of course. Particular consideration has been given to the integration of technological systems able to optimise the building's sustainability in energy terms. For example, the use of solar and photovoltaic panels on the roof, the collection and recovery of rainwater (all the areas of vegetation will be equipped with automated systems of irrigation using recovered rainwater) and the production of geothermal energy.

Bosconavigli can be considered paradigmatic in its exploration of the synergy between the architectural scale and the urban one through the presence of vegetation, which here provides the link between these two dimensions. How do these two scales interact in the project and in relation to the city's schemes of green regeneration?

All 90 of the apartments in Bosconavigli – varying in size from 45 to over 300 sqm – include large outdoor spaces, conceived as an extension of the indoor ones, true 'open-air rooms'. In addition to providing a high quality of accommodation, loggias and terraces represent the main element in the design of the elevations, articulated on the basis of their orientation. The fronts onto the internal courtyard are characterised by a pattern of loggias, a play of voids and solids designed to provide protection from the sun in the summer and favour it in the winter. The fronts that hold a dialogue with the urban fabric, on the other hand, are distinguished by an irregular alternating set of balconies, designed to hold plants and tall trees, that provide a barrier against noise and particulate pollution and favour an increase in biodiversity and a general improvement in the building's energy performance. And then the project is set at the centre of a system of parks and gardens and public pathways: around the building extend a park of 3,500 sqm for condominial use, with sports facilities and recreation activities, a regenerated public area of over 7,800 sqm and the future Linear Park along the bed of the disused railway.

Through a series of projects, your practice has introduced and tested a number of solutions in which nature has become an integral part of architectural and urban design. After all these years, what point has your research reached? What are the parameters that have been established and the ones still to be explored?

The project of the Bosco Verticale was the first prototype of a new kind of architecture, the first building in which the relationship with living nature was considered a fundamental criterion of the design. For this reason, it was for us a genuine experiment that today, almost ten years after its construction, has turned out well. At the same time, it was not a point of arrival, but of departure: a case study that has constantly given us the possibility to understand, study and, as a consequence, improve various aspects of this new architectural model. It has been a great 'school' for us, a lesson in experimenting and innovating, precisely because the research connected with a building like this has a very important role in monitoring the growth of the project and looking at the next steps.

Currently the firm is working on several interventions that are exploring the dialogue between nature and architecture, by now in very different parts of the world.

At present our firm, Stefano Boeri Architetti, is working on 77 projects in 28 countries. One of the first steps we have taken is to focus on experimentation in dry climates, studying the possibility of introducing plants that can withstand conditions of greater aridity, and taking up the challenge of responding to the exigencies of the climate in the part of the world that is suffering most as a result of climate changes. Our plans for the Vertical Forest in Dubai, presented at COP27, and the Vertical Forest in Cairo are examples of these efforts to integrate the environmental benefits of urban forestation with the problems of water management and extreme climatic conditions.

Back in Milan, on the other hand, we are thinking of ways for the Bosco Verticale to house photovoltaic panels to produce electric power on the roof and the façades – as we did in the case of Pirelli 39, also in the Porta Nuova area.

Research and experimentation on the relationship between city, nature, and architecture, however, has become one of your strongpoints, almost a mark of identity, that goes beyond the confines of the individual intervention and takes a broader view of the project, on a regional scale.

Yes, our 'obsession' with greenery has also led us to propose a vision that takes account of the whole of the country's green heritage, that of the big cities as well as the small and medium-sized towns, connecting it up and creating a national park – along the lines of Richard Weller's World Park. There are forests in Italy, but we have not yet learnt how to utilise them in a productive way. The Parco Italia project, developed by our Department of Research and presented at the second World Forum on Urban Forests in Washington DC, envisages a system of ecological corridors that criss-cross the peninsula from north to south and from east to west, uniting existing parks with protected areas and unprotected wooded areas, including a renewed constellation of small towns, villages and metropolitan areas that will be able to meet the challenge of the integration of nature into the urban panorama. Not a simple challenge but one that needs to be taken up as soon as possible. This would create a grand unified system that would lead to the planting of 22 million new trees in the space of a few years, about one tree for each inhabitant of the 14 cities involved: a number that, if extended to towns with a population of over 15,000, could reach 60 million. With these figures, it would be possible to achieve a profound improvement in public health by absorbing 250-400 tonnes of carbon dioxide a year, promoting national and transnational environmental connections, countering climate change and fostering the ecological transition.

Green welfare

Nature as a source of well-being in the workplace

The topic of a changing environment and climate, and its socio-cultural consequences, has had a direct effect on many areas of our daily lives, urging us to come up with ideas and solutions in order to deal with it in an appropriate manner. In particular, the work sector has had to invest in searching for new strategies of growth and renewing its spaces in terms of quality and welfare services. While a transformation had already gotten underway in the last few years, we are now faced with a real revolution following the long period of forced smart working. The changes brought by the pandemic have made it even more urgent to provide people with places where the sense of well-being and the value generated by the spaces in which they work are absolutely transparent and tangible.

Indoor spaces, but also and above all outdoor areas, sometimes large but more often small in size, and in many cases still undervalued, in which, through nature, it is possible to try out projects and solutions aimed at a general improvement in the quality of working life. The objective is to design more hospitable workplaces, but also spaces for interaction, for representation, for meeting or working in groups; spaces to hold large and small events, in pleasant settings where there is a complete continuity between inside and outside.

This tangible and concrete response is what AG&P greenscape has dubbed 'green welfare'.

Over the course of the research and work carried out in recent years, four tendencies have been identified in the corporate sector, which today is still in need of a fair amount of evolution and transformation. The first tendency concerns the new business districts. More and more often parks and gardens are at the centre of new interventions of urban regeneration, in order to provide residents, and workers too, with easy access to more agreeable environments.

To take one example among many, Porta Nuova in Milan, the first urban district in the world to have been certified as sustainable. The whole intervention is laid out around a central park, the Biblioteca degli Alberi (Library of Trees), which provides the opportunity for a revitalising moment for residents and for all the people who pass through or work in this area every day, crossing the park or using it to take a break before and after work. Another district in Milan that has been developed along similar lines to Porta Nuova is CityLife, where the CityWave project by BIG (Bjarke Ingels Group) is under construction. AG&P greenscape is supervising the executive project of the open spaces, adopting this concept of nature as a welfare resource and developing it further. All the areas of this private intervention are open to use by the public, with a view to optimisation of the relationship between the public and private spheres in urban dynamics.

The possibility of making the open spaces in new urban interventions permeable and welcoming makes the city a more liveable and accessible place, from the perspective of a great quality of the working environment as well. These are new and exemplary neighbourhoods, stemming from the collaboration between public and private, in which nature is at the very heart of the planning process, and the functions laid out around it, such as offices and housing, benefit from these open spaces of high quality with abundant services.

The second tendency is linked instead with those businesses that have the possibility to devote space to what are known as 'company parks'. This category includes projects of broad scope and on a large scale. Areas of great size that are being reclaimed and placed at the disposal of employees and their families, and often the local community as well. In recent years AG&P greenscape has been given the opportunity to tackle this theme in some interesting projects.

For instance, Crédit Agricole's new Green Life headquarters in Parma, where the park has become a genuine added value of company welfare, utilised by all the staff and, at the weekend, their families too, as well as being open to the public for more cultural occasions and moments of social exchange. Or the park of the new Siemens headquarters in Milan, which offers a variety of settings, including spaces devoted to relaxation, sport, and socialisation, along with a part set aside for vegetable gardens that are tended by employees. It is open to their families at weekends and to the people of the city on more public and social occasions.

It has been extensively demonstrated that plants can help reduce stress, increase the attention span and generally improve well-being, which in turn boosts productivity.

Utilising them in an intelligent and sensitive way is unquestionably a new challenge for the corporate sector.

The third tendency regards spaces of industrial or craft production, located in or outside major urban centres, that are reutilised with a view to urban regeneration and, potentially, can be turned into new workplaces designed based on more innovative concepts of well-being. The Gucci brand is a prime example of these processes of urban regeneration of manufacturing sectors. In recent years the company has been investing a great deal to provide more welcoming open spaces where employees' well-being is the focus of the design as an added value for the company. This shows how spaces for work can be reconsidered today in relation to changes in ways of working.

More welcoming and informal environments, of higher quality, in which the time spent by people, including their free time, becomes essential to their well-being, are increasingly necessary and sought after; places where reconnecting with nature can only be an added value.

On the previous page: view of the Crédit Agricole Green Life park in Parma.

On this page, right and below: two views of the Gucci Hub project in Milan.

Right: the park of the Siemens Italia headquarters in Milan. Below: the Flying Wood inside the entrance hall of the Allianz Italia headquarters in Milan.

However, constraints on the budget and the space available do not always allow the creation of such large open areas. At times it is necessary to deal with smaller spaces, set in urban fabrics of greater density, on the scale of the single building. Nature was once viewed in the corporate world as a sort of interior decoration, often reserved for just a few spaces.

Today, instead, it is increasingly common to find in offices what AG&P greenscape calls 'pocket gardens', the fourth of these tendencies: external spaces often complementary to the buildings that house them.

By exploiting even quite small areas, it is possible to create gardens that may be of reduced dimensions but in which nature can still be the protagonist.

In the Pocket Campus of the head offices of the Compagnia di San Paolo in Turin, for example, the studio has sought to unite two complementary concepts: the campus, as a shared space of exchange, and the pocket size, on the scale of a small urban space. Created on the bed of a car park that has been turned into a garden, the Pocket Campus is a completely new kind of setting, designed to be in total continuity with the internal spaces.

Equipped with the necessary technology, it is a place in which it is possible to work, hold meetings and stage conferences, in a group or alone; a garden that is also a place of representation, the manifesto of a collective well-being, inside and outside the building.

The same concept has been applied in the garden of the office complex at Via Monte Rosa 91, designed by the RPBW in 1998 and now renovated by the same firm, where the existing plaza and patch of woodland, located at the centre of the internal courtyard, have become the new beating heart of the intervention. The wood has been transformed by insertions made in a discreet and respectful manner, through suspended walkways that have made it possible to work on the layer of undergrowth and enrich it with new colours and scents, making it a pleasant place to be whatever the season: an accessible and permeable place where it is also possible to work thanks to the technology with which it is equipped. The plaza, in turn, is designed to be more accessible and open to the public too. It is dotted with islands of vegetation, which have replaced parts of the paving and turned them into open-air rooms, patches of colour and fragrance, agreeable and shaded areas.

The four tendencies, which cover interventions on quite different scales, are helping to reinforce a diffused landscape that is playing an ever more fundamental part in our city, and that should make its way into all the spheres and spaces of our lives, both outdoors and indoors.

So, it is important to be able to create spaces of connection, places immersed in nature in which people can meet, interact, hang out and even work, benefiting from the sense of well-being produced by plants and natural settings.

Today the world of business has grasped the potential of nature as a tool to produce welfare for its employees and give added value not only to its own community, but also to the city as a whole.

HQ Fondazione Compagnia di San Paolo Pocket Campus Bernini, Turin

The Pocket Campus project, built in the outer courtyard of Palazzo Bernini on part of an area designated for parking, is a long, natural oasis in a densely built-up context, protected from other pre-existing structures by natural and architectural elements. A small park for private use, with spaces for relaxation, socialising, and moments of work in the open air.

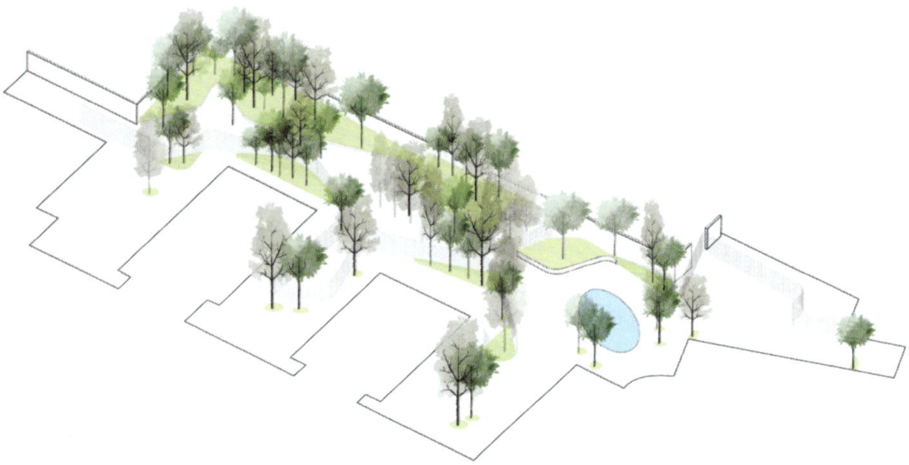

Via Monte Rosa 91, Milan

The Monte Rosa 91 complex is now undergoing its second transformation, entrusted once again to the hands of RPBW. The concept of transparency and openness guides the new intervention, with the aim of offering a multifunctional space, in which the park becomes an open oasis that can be crossed during daylight hours, an integral part of the urban fabric and the city life of the neighbourhood.

On these pages: above: a summary overview of the flora and fauna in the park project; below: two images of the project.

On the next page: one of the paths in the Green Life park in Parma.

Edifici Aria-Energia-Luce

Crédit Agricole Green Life, Parma

The design of Crédit Agricole Green Life's Arboretum Park, at the renovated headquarters of the banking group in Parma, presented an opportunity to experiment creatively with the relationship with nature as a fundamental component of corporate welfare. In fact the park generates an extensive system of open spaces of great landscape and environmental quality, rich in content and in possibilities of different uses for the bank's employees. A place for recreation, socialisation, and physical activity in contact with nature, it is in line with the development of the new offices, designed to facilitate meeting and sharing and modelled around people's well-being.

Over 500 new trees, along with thousands of shrubs and ornamental plants, form a green lung covering more than 7 hectares. Of great environmental value for the whole region, it can bear comparison with the main parks of the city in terms of its size, biomass, and high degree of biodiversity. The landscape design of the new green areas upholds the criteria adopted by the Frigerio Design Group's project of expansion of the service centre.

The large park that surrounds the buildings is divided into several different areas, such as the Giardino dei Fiori, the Anfiteatro Verde, the Viale dei Pioppi, and the large Arboretum. All these places are laid out around the new piazza, key location of the project and main gateway of entrance to the park, as well as the hinge between it, the old building, and the newly constructed ones.

Dialogue with the team

Emanuele Bortolotti, Paolo Palmulli, Alessandro Battaglia , Sofya Dolgaya, Barbara Mariani, Lucia Nadalin, Marco Nelli, Pierpaolo Tagliola

More and more companies are investing in green spaces for their employees. How do you tackle the design of a corporate park today?

Paolo Today's digitalisation has enabled us to separate work from a fixed location and established hours. This aspect has brought about great changes in the sector and has made it possible to transform and modify the concept of open spaces in terms of the presence of nature as an added value of a new idea of fringe benefits for employees, integrated with all the other services provided. In each project, the objective is to create open spaces as an important natural resource, for the company and for local residents. After only a few years since the first works, we are already seeing substantial results. The quality of a project is also judged over time, by the experience of those who live in it: Crédit Agricole's Arboretum Park, which opened in 2019, is a good example. It is a much-utilised space, an integral part of company life. People have welcomed it and made it their own. It is sufficient to see what happens at lunchtime when the weather is good!

Emanuele Crédit Agricole is a project of proper landscaping, and complex too. The company's headquarters is located on the outskirts of the city of Parma and has been extended by the Frigerio Group studio, maintaining the existing building designed by Vico Magistretti, at the time for Cariparma, which had already been enriched by the presence of a large area of parkland.

How did you tackle the dialogue between the new and the existing building in this project?

Emanuele The idea was developed based on three main guidelines: the first of a landscaping type, the second of a regulatory type and the third one of environmental sustainability as well as the well-being of employees. Landscaping, since we had to fit into the surrounding area, which was once farmland and is almost urban today, integrating the new structure with the existing one and with the open space that was already there. Regulatory, because to build the new headquarters we were obliged to plant, as a compensation, at least 700 trees. Environmental sustainability and employee welfare have allowed us to approach this park with new models and solutions. Living and working in contact with nature is an added value today. The new offices have been conceived in such a way that the surrounding landscape would not just be scenery in the background, but a place to live in.

So, it is a park equipped with some sort of facilities.

Paolo Yes, we have included amenities that can be used for leisure activities by the 1,500 employees of Crédit Agricole during their free time, such as sports facilities and spaces for socialising, creativity, events, and performances, as well as for team building or open-air meetings.

How was the project developed in relation to the existing building?

Emanuele There are two elements that have led the design of the park: Magistretti's existing axis, which extended with its black poplars towards the park from the old headquarters, and the signs left by the Roman centuriation of the fields, a feature typical of the Emilian countryside.

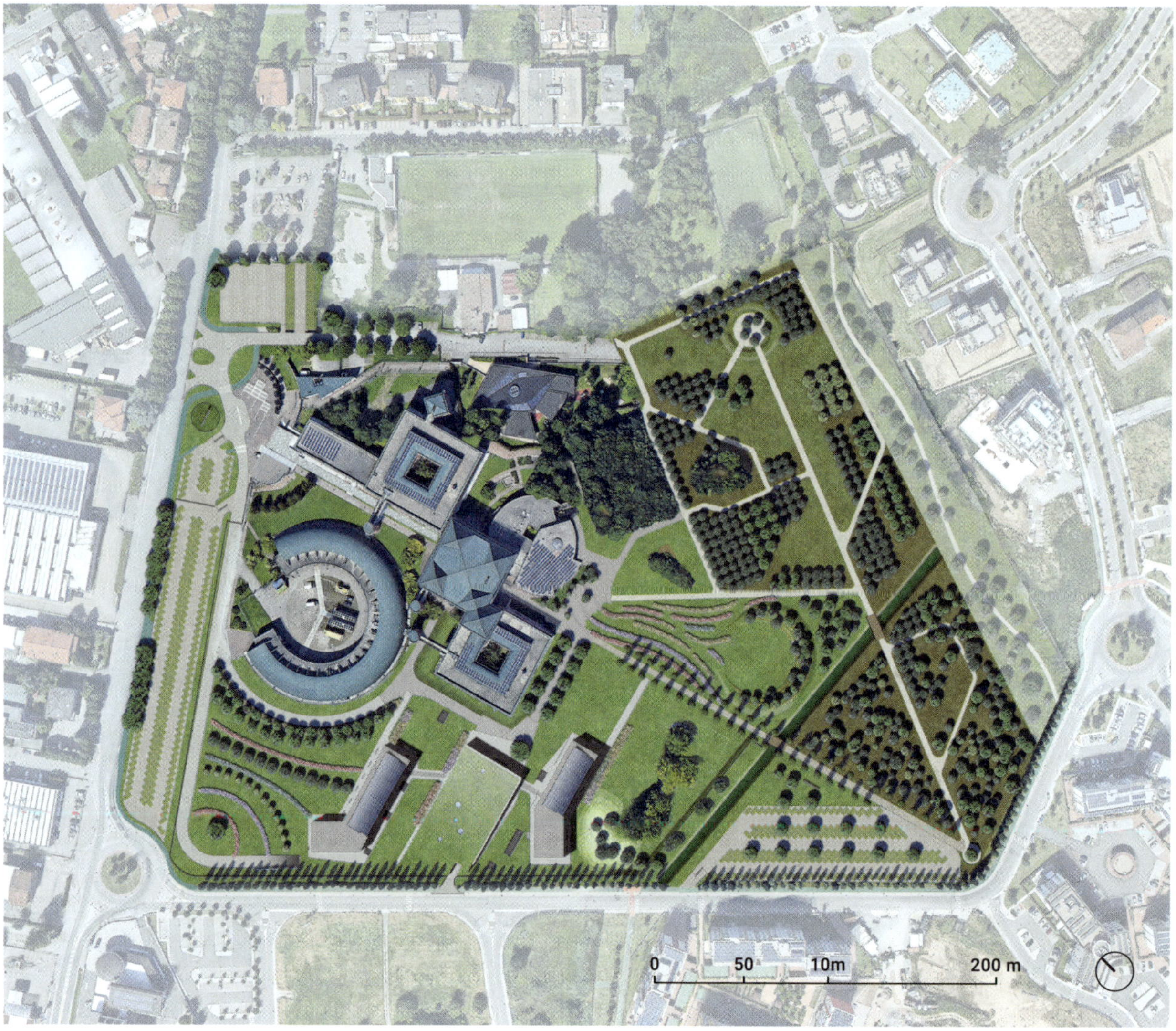

On this page: plan of the park project.
Facing page: view from above of the park.

Facing page: employees socialising in the park.
On this page: a view of the Anfiteatro Verde.

On the following pages: some glimpses of the park and an outdoor workstation.

We distributed the 700 trees we had to plant along these marks, creating arboreta, groups of trees of the same kind arranged in blocks to create a setting and a more varied environment. In the area where these trees are located, there are also clay paths, to be used for various activities, from sports to recreation.

At the centre, instead, lies the heart of the park known as Anfiteatro Verde, with the Giardino dei Fiori and the Piazza. Fields filled with flowers alternate with large expanse of lawn. This is the first park in Italy where there is a large area set aside for grass, whose maintenance is carried out by solar-powered robots, which cut the grass and reuse it as organic material, without any need to take it away. The Piazza, on the other hand, is not only the main entrance of the park, but also acts as a hinge between it, the old building and the ones that have just been constructed. It has a more mineral character, with paving that has a pattern recalling cracked soil and seats that play with geometries to create a space that is always different.

What was it like to manage a construction site with many different specialised site managers?

Alessandro The construction site for the park was an exciting experience. Managing many stakeholders involved (client, construction management, specialised professionals, contractors, subcontractors, etc.) was a real challenge. The team worked cohesively and synergistically from the first day until the final acceptance. Our constant presence on site allowed us to keep a good pace of execution, and it was possible to deliver the different areas in the various scheduled steps. It was also fascinating to see all the Crédit Agricole employees occupy the park and enjoy it between working and relaxing moments.

As Paolo was saying, the quality of a project becomes apparent over time, examining how it is lived and used by those who inhabit it. How has the park been welcomed by the employees?

Emanuele Very well. Let me give you an example: we initially tried inserting a geometric platform in the groups of trees, to serve as a small wired-up meeting area in the midst of greenery, to test its use during work hours as well, for those who like to carry out some of their assignments outdoors; it was so popular that there are now seven of these platforms.

So, is it a very well lived park?

Emanuele The park today is a green organism, lush with vegetation. There are over a thousand shrubs and perennials: the Giardino dei Fiori alone has around eight hundred. And it is full of spaces for meeting, socialising, and exchanging ideas. An active, lively, and much used place, able to lift people's spirits and provide them with pleasant settings in which to relax or work. The Giardino dei Fiori, for example, has been designed to have flowers in bloom during almost every month of the year (except for December and January). In addition, a small refreshment point has been set up inside the Arboretum, a gathering place and attraction for the people who are making this place their own.

Apart from the one at Crédit Agricole, the studio has carried out and is still working on other projects offering employees the fringe benefit of a green space. What are the different ways in which you have been working in this sector?

Pierpaolo It depends on the spaces at our disposal. For instance, Crédit Agricole's Arboretum is the one on the largest scale, an agricultural park, an open-air setting where it is possible to go for walks as if it were a section of countryside, something of incredible value for a company! Siemens' Park, which gives a nod to this kind of layout, is of a fair size, but the area is more compact. For Gucci in Novara, we have created a small and sheltered area of vegetation in a very built-up setting. And the Pocket Campus of Palazzo Bernini, which in my view is the prototype of a project based on green welfare and the provision of greenery as a benefit for employees. It involved the transformation of a courtyard used as a car park, somewhat hemmed in by the dense urban fabric of Turin, into a place where nature is taking over again.

Il Noce

Barbara These works show how today the green welfare project has also become a way to convey those values in which companies recognise themselves, integrating two important aspects: making employees live better, but also interpreting the customer's identity. It is increasingly evident how the design of nature in open spaces has also become part of the construction of the client's brand identity.

When you think of nature, what you always have in mind is something unspoilt, whereas it emerges very clearly from the works of the studio that this nature must indeed be nurtured, but also carefully designed. You study techniques and technologies and develop them to provide specific solutions.

Marco Technology allows us to introduce what we consider to be nature in difficult contexts. We use technology to put vegetation where it would not theoretically be possible for it to exist. Green terraces and roofs and green walls are two of the most technological solutions we have to take vegetation into difficult contexts and are the subject of continuous research and technological innovation.

What solutions did you adopt in the Pocket Campus?

Marco In the Pocket Campus we have used green terraces and roofs, and have removed the floor from two areas, replacing it with a permeable surface. When such solutions are adopted, it is necessary to know which plants to utilise, and here the expertise of the designer comes into play, to see what is the best solution for the choice of plant species to use.

The Siemens Park, on the other hand, has been deliberately conceived with its own means of access, precisely to make it more accessible to the employees and their families independently of the company's opening hours.

Sofya That's right. The concept of employee welfare has been broadened to suit the needs of people and their families. The new park is conceived as a space for work but also for recreation, sport, and play, with dedicated areas whose character and design vary. The vegetation chosen is rich and varied and includes plants that bear fruit.

Lucia This shows how more and more companies are choosing to provide their employees with spaces that are not just for show, linked to communication or marketing strategies. Instead, the importance of the quality of people's working life has slowly been understood at a more profound level. Thus, open spaces, as well as more informal spaces for sharing various moments, both work and leisure, take on an important role thanks also to the presence of nature. And this new approach becomes even more interesting when some of these open spaces are also created for the use of families.

The true wealth of Siemens's Park is in fact the involvement of employees in the activities and in the discovery and exploration of the park.

Sofya Exactly so! In fact, illustrative panels have also been set up in the park to illustrate the names of the different areas and how they can be used, to inform employees about the different species of plants in the park, to show how they change with the seasons and to relate the history of the project as well. There are a small greenhouse and a vegetable garden, which are tended by the employees themselves.

Can we say that nature and the landscape have played a key role in helping changes that were already underway concerning the theme of well-being in the workplace?

Emanuele Certainly! Nature is the key factor that can make the difference compared to normal architectural solutions. It is a concept that we had already begun to explore but that we have really been able to visualise and test in recent years, and we are already seeing great results. The direction is undoubtedly the right one.

The quality of new work spaces: investing in the landscape

Conversation with

Crédit Agricole Italia

The concept of 'corporate welfare' has evolved a great deal in recent years. Work environments are now more dynamic spaces, dedicated to meetings and dialogue between people, introducing new parameters of quality and well-being. Deciding to invest in welfare by creating a large space for its employees dedicated to nature was a great challenge, almost a pioneering one. How did the idea of building the park come about?

CA Green Life is a tangible example of how Crédit Agricole wanted to invest in welfare, combining respect for the environment and innovation with the element of socialisation and well-being for employees.

The park was inaugurated in 2018 as an eco-sustainable and state-of-the-art space, with the aim of creating areas able to promote a new working philosophy. A modern 12,000 sqm multifunctional centre, housing around 1,400 employees, set in a park with 70,000 sqm of greenery, and with buildings that reflect the highest green building standards.

Various initiatives have been undertaken to date to improve conditions for our employees. From workstations arranged in multifunctional open-plan spaces to technologically advanced meeting rooms, and from the 450-seat company canteen to the 400-seat main auditorium, every single building at CA is structured in such a way as to shorten distances and work as a team, so that getting to know people and exchanging skills is always encouraged. At the same time, work-life balance policies are promoted through a variety of tools: from smart working, the provision of laptops and state-of-the-art communication technologies, to services such as a company crèche, laundry, tailoring, grocery delivery, tyre change, parcel pick-up or a take-away service to plan for one's evening meal.

With the Green Life park, the Group aims to reinforce its commitment to sustainability, a commitment that has been nurtured and solidified over time through various conscientious initiatives undertaken in full awareness of the importance of safeguarding the environment: the use of durable and recyclable materials for the construction of new buildings; the introduction of the concept of sensory comfort for optimising the quality of spaces in terms of hygrothermal, acoustic and lighting conditions; and the attention to energy saving implemented with the use of integrated systems and solutions for the on-site production of energy from renewable sources.

Making such a large park available to employees proved to be a fortunate intuition in pre-Covid times, and it was consistent with the desire of investing in social relationships, inside and outside our offices, adopting a horizontal approach as opposed to the vertical vision brought about by offices in skyscrapers.

In recent years, the park has hosted internal and external events, conventions and institutional and convivial moments, appreciated by all guests and experienced fully by all employees.

An increasing number of studies show the improvement in people's psychological and physical well-being and productivity when in contact with nature. Even more so if there is the possibility of also being able to work surrounded by nature. How have the ways of working and the use of the park by employees changed in its early years?

In recent years, the Crédit Agricole Italia Group has chosen to go beyond the consolidated concept of traditional welfare, broadening it towards the concept of well-being, with the aim of increasingly benefiting the work-life balance of all employees.

The opening of Green Life in Parma marked a clear and decisive change in the working habits of Crédit Agricole Italia employees. Among the many benefits provided is the possibility of using the park surrounding the buildings, where employees can spend their breaks, strolling and relaxing in a green space of over seven hectares comprising more than 500 trees, thousands of hedges, ornamental plants and a flower garden.

It is an uncommon privilege to be able to use these spaces to carry out one's usual work activities, such as holding meetings, team meetings and discussions in the open air, taking advantage of the benefits of natural light. It is well known that working in close contact with nature reduces stress, increases productivity and stimulates innovation as well as creativity, allowing a higher degree of concentration, increased energy and consequently a much better quality of working life. Being able to work in Green Life's spaces also increases people's level of well-being. Tables and benches are transformed into new desks and the park's paths into corridors for moving between offices. On many occasions, the spaces also become social gathering places, used for numerous events, enabling new acquaintances and improving interpersonal relations between colleagues. Over the years, we have found that the first to appreciate the new ways of working at CA Green Life are the employees themselves. What not long ago seemed like a difficult framework to develop has now become the norm.

Having a park at hand during working hours, and the opportunity to spend time in contact with nature also promotes a greater awareness of the value and importance of safeguarding the natural environment around us. Can the Green Life park be considered a kind of sustainability manifesto of your corporate identity?

CA Green Life is the tangible expression of our sustainability-oriented philosophy. For the Group, environmental issues play a key role. So much so, indeed, that they represent one of the three pillars of our Medium-term Plan 22-25, together with innovation and digitalisation. Sustainability characterises all our business lines and represents a global performance factor, as well as a tool with which to accompany customers towards the energy-environment transition. In concrete terms, the Group's strategy aims to promote a low-carbon economy, accelerating the advent of renewable energies and abandonment of fossil fuels, and to support a transition in the agri-food sector, fostering a competitive agricultural and food system that protects biodiversity and preserves natural capital. We also aim to strengthen social cohesion and inclusion, enhancing the potential of territories and bringing young people closer to the world of work, while respecting gender diversity.

Therefore sustainability underpins your initiatives and activities to support environmental preservation in all its broadest aspects?

Certainly. In Italy, with our ESG (Environmental, Social, Governance) plan, we can absolutely consider sustainability an identifying factor of our activities. So much so that we have integrated it throughout the bank's value chain in line with a holistic view of the three pillars, for each of which precise governance is defined. In lending, for example, climate issues are included in the risk assessment, for both physical and transitional risks, in both appraisal and granting practices. A service model is in place whereby we offer green products to the Private, Agricultural, Food and Corporate Bank markets, such as those that incentivise the energy transition of buildings and sustainable mobility. We provide ad hoc financing lines for companies that have already embarked on a path towards sustainability, in order to support them in improving their business processes on ESG aspects, alongside specialised ESG advice in Wealth Management.

To conclude, our commitment to environmental protection is set in stone and has the goal of achieving zero net emissions by 2050. In Europe, we are the leading private financier and the leading institutional investor in renewable energies, as well as the leading player in the issuance of Green, Sustainability & Social Bonds, with a wide range of green loans and funds. CA wants to be a benchmark in the energy transition path and we are convinced that only by reorienting the business towards ESG will we turn risks into opportunities and generate value for society.

Heritage

Re-imagining and enhancing the natural, architectural and urban heritage through landscape design

The European Landscape Convention of 2000 expressed very clearly how landscape must be considered as the result of the action of natural and human factors and their interaction, and therefore, expanding the concept, as a manifestation of the bond that identifies each society with the space in which it develops. And it is precisely this interpretation that, far beyond a purely aesthetic and formal conception, confirms the need to consider the landscape as heritage, supported by appropriate planning and management, in the integration of its components, and focused on the role it plays in the memory and identity of society. However, in some cases – for various historical, environmental, or socio-economic reasons – parks, gardens, monuments, or entire portions of cities have been neglected, abandoned to decay, destined for (or besieged by) inappropriate uses, compromising the synergic and vital relationship with the context and communities.

This major yet betrayed heritage can be recovered and revalued while at the same time pursuing other compelling objectives, such as improving quality of life, safeguarding human rights and sustainable development, adapting this heritage to the spirit of the present time.

The key to interpreting landscape in terms of heritage should be seen as a kind of evolution that goes beyond the view of heritage itself as an exceptional art-historical phenomenon and accepts its relational and cultural dimension. In line with this approach, heritage takes on a *raison d'être* to the extent that it is associated with an existing urban or natural landscape, recognised and enjoyed by communities, which defines and contextualises it. And thus, it is no longer conceived as a mere object to be preserved, but as a perceived value to be enjoyed and cared for.

Accepting that heritage is shaped by a social process implies that it is not something given once and for all, but is a social construct, in which it is not a matter of identifying specific tangible entities, with precise limits or elective parameters, but of detecting its values, and also of introducing the variable of time, which makes it a product with an evolutionary and transformative dimension.

Formulas based on the definition of protective perimeters and restrictive criteria are totally insufficient to deal with this dynamic condition. The very concept of protection used for urban parks, for example, is to be understood broadly, if parks include a natural component that is itself constantly changing, and a human component whose needs and desires change over time. It is clear, therefore, how necessary it is to develop a different, dynamic and above all adaptive strategy that considers monumental systems as palimpsests that have been composed by layering both built elements and open, more or less natural, spaces over time, together with the experience produced by the interrelation between them and people.

The protection of the landscape heritage cannot be based on simple conservation: instead, it is necessary to focus processes, projects, and interventions on controlling the transformations that take place there (and which are necessary and part of an evolutionary growth of places), so as not to compromise its identity values. Redesigning, enhancing, and improving the quality of use and understanding of the natural, architectural and urban heritage remains the primary objective of any landscape intervention.

The choice between conservation or development is outdated and ineffective. Landscape is, on the contrary, a strategic factor from which to build a renewed and careful management of the natural or built heritage based on the principles of sustainable development and adaptive transformations. The issue of safeguarding the existing is equally important, as is enhancement through modernisation of existing historical landscapes. Today, safeguarding means re-evaluating, giving renewed significance and improving the quality of existing landscapes to return them to the urban fabric and its citizens in a contemporary way.

With this general principle regarding the role of the landscape project in the enhancement of heritage, interpreted through a more synergetic and contemporary view, the studio has carried out several projects for the transformation and renovation of parks, gardens, or public spaces, of the most diverse dimensions and uses. There are two main project thrusts: on the one hand, the commitment to the promotion of historic gardens and parks that have already been protected or specifically recognised: the heritage landscapes; on the other hand, the transformation and provision of new significance to open spaces that are closely related to monumental, architectural or urban presences, whose value is compromised by a degraded or poor quality context: the heritage sites' landscapes .

The primary objective for all interventions is to protect existing elements of value and at the same time respectfully update the landscape palimpsest with integrations consistent with bio-climatic and social evolution, under the banner of a more sustainable and aware approach.

As far as heritage landscapes are concerned, projects have been designed and implemented, for example, to restore the gardens of Villa Rezzola in Lerici, the garden of Palazzo Clerici in Milan, the gardens of the Zacchera Hotels on Lake Maggiore, the reuse of the garden of the Rinnovata Pizzigoni School in Milan and the park of the Santa Maria della Pietà complex in Rome. Carefully safeguarding the historic natural heritage, the interventions were oriented towards supporting and strengthening the existing greenery by inserting a few elements to seal in its importance and enhancement, while also integrating new uses and spaces more appropriate to them.

On the other hand, looking at heritage sites' landscapes, one of the most important interventions carried out in recent years has been on an important historical and symbolic place:

On the previous page: an aerial view of the Palazzo in Parco Te, and of the new intervention in the background. On this page: two views and a photo-simulation of Villa Rezzola, an ancient mansion protected by FAI, in Lerici.

Above and below, left: two images of gardens and views of the Zacchera Hotels on Lake Maggiore.
Below, right: a view of the garden of the new premises of the Pinacoteca di Brera at Palazzo Citterio in Milan.

the site of Palazzo Te in Mantua, protected as a cultural heritage site by UNESCO. To intervene on such a remarkable area required an in-depth and specific research process, study, and design.

Being able to reconstruct the history of heritage sites' landscapes, whether protected or not, and making sense of the different changes that have taken place over time, are fundamental aspects to ensure that interventions and related conservation, management and re-signification actions are appropriate. In this way, it is possible to direct planning towards a more conscious protection, enhancing the significant aspects of a landscape and inserting more contemporary uses that are attentive to the historical and cultural context.

A symbolic place for the inhabitants of Mantua, the site of Palazzo Te has endured through centuries and arrived at the recent past considerably transformed and besieged by incoherent functions and spaces of poor quality. The main duty in intervening on such a sensitive monumental complex was to seek a new balance making it possible to preserve and at the same time regenerate the meaning and sense of a landscape, while also adapting it to contemporary uses. This is how the project for the recovery and transformation of a large area that had lost a significant relationship with the Palazzo over the years and housed various sports and service functions was approached. The design process, in concert and in constant and open dialogue with the public administration and various other entities, was triggered by the desire to protect the historical heritage in combination with a strong desire to create an area capable of interpreting the citizens' requests for an equipped urban public park, according to the principle that 'the city belongs to those who live in it'.

By adopting spatial solutions that recall the geometries of the Italian garden and emphasise the monumental presence of the Palazzo, preserving the existing plants and integrating a rich combination of newly planted vegetation, inserting new paths and functions more suited to today's vitality and social dynamics, the result is an urban park of new generation, with a hybrid and surprising character, connected and in open dialogue with the city and its context.

It is a place full of life, experienced during the day as well as in the evening, completely regenerated and returned to the daily life of a city that has been able to believe in and enhance such an important landscape heritage with foresight, while looking to the future.

A similar approach was also used in the design of the master plan for the enhancement of the Fortezza del Priamar and its context, in Savona. In this case, the project has taken into account the historical and archaeological features as well as the pre-existing trees, and the monumental complex has been placed at the centre of a new park that recomposes and transforms a mosaic of underused or poor-quality spaces. This is in line with a unified long-term vision that can be achieved in stages, affecting spaces inside and outside the historical walls and creating new gardens, terraces, and special places to encourage the re-appropriation of the city's symbolic monument by its inhabitants.

The theme of reuse and renewing the significance of a heritage site, even and especially when protected, is one of the key challenges for contemporary and future landscape design and is of particular importance for the heritage site itself and its users, in relation to a variety of issues concerning accessibility and usability; education, contextualisation and interpretation; preservation and protection; appropriation by communities; aesthetic, economic and cultural enhancement; and last but not least, environmental sustainability, considering the possibility for these places to strengthen their role in terms of offering ecosystem services.

Using this perspective to interpret a landscape project for heritage will ensure the challenges of its management are addressed more effectively, allowing the regeneration of the values of a site to be built around present and future generations that will live and look after it.

Parco del Priamar, Savona

The master plan for the enhancement of the Fortezza del Priamar and the spaces around it, leveraging existing practices and the existing historical, archaeological and arboreal features, reconsiders the monumental complex as the heart of a new park that extends inside and outside its walls: a collection of gardens, terraces and special places that facilitate the re-appropriation by citizens of this monumental asset, through an increase in the presence of nature.

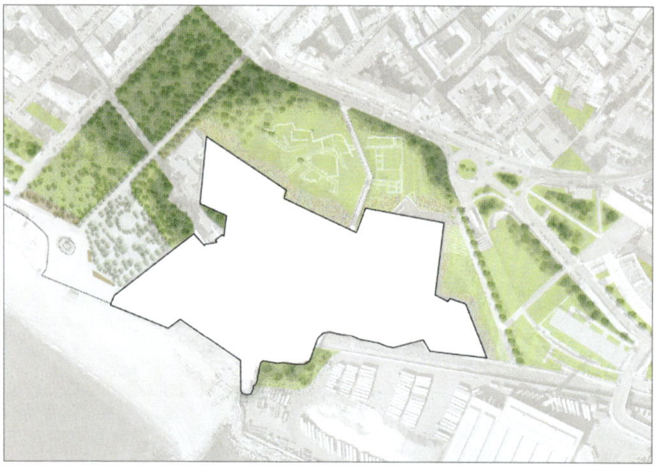

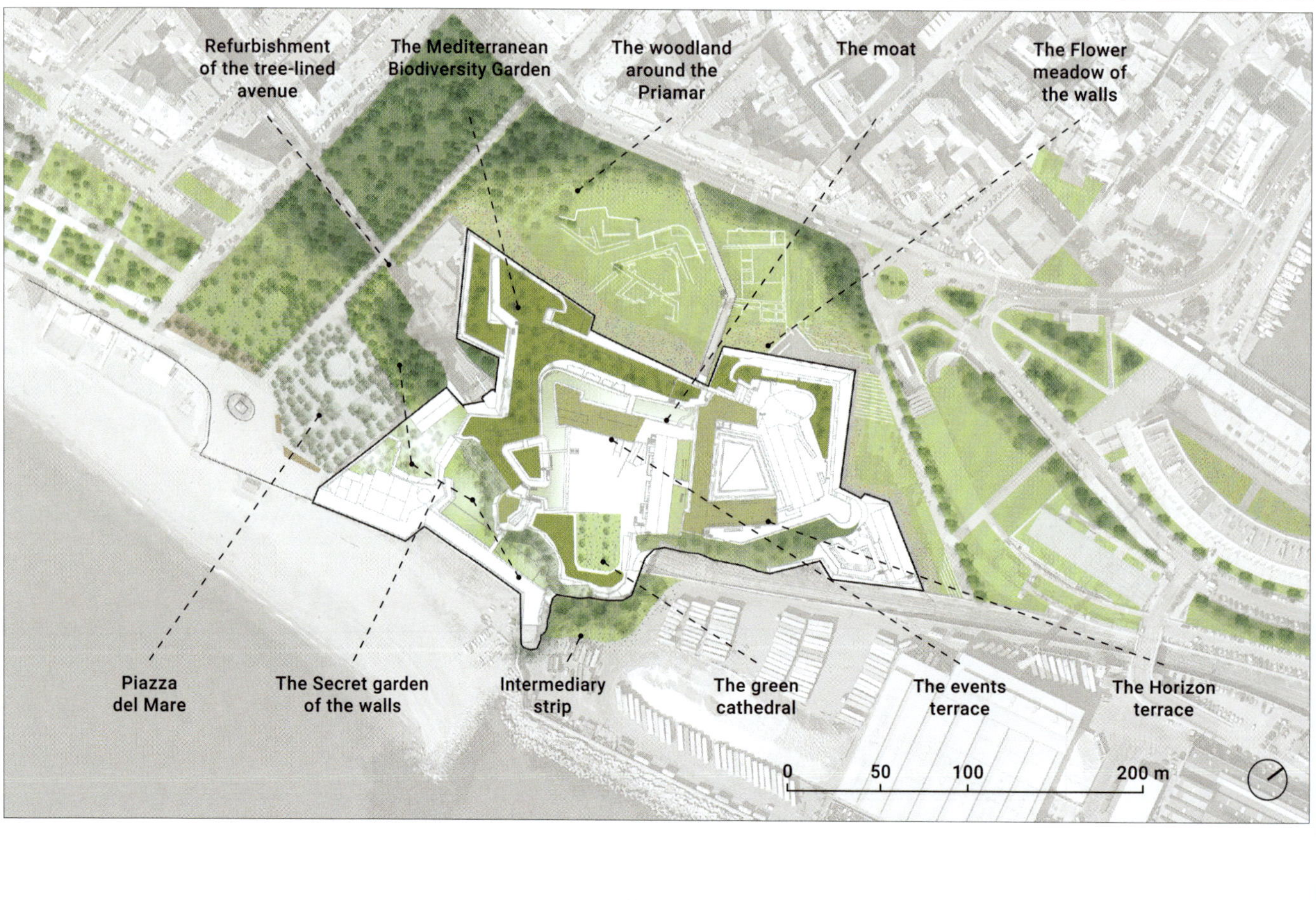

Rinnovata Pizzigoni School, Milan

The school, founded in 1927, is a reference model for the management of educational environments, in which open space and nature are an integral part of teaching. The garden renovation project partially reorganises the existing area for animals and the vegetable garden, and enriches the spaces with different circular, didactic and play environments.

On this page: aerial view of the Palazzo Te project. On the following page: a photo of the park.

Parco Te, Mantua

The Parco Te project in Mantua combines two substantial features: the protection of the historical heritage, on the one hand, due to the presence of Palazzo Te within the area (the historical monument and, indeed, the whole area, are protected by UNESCO) and its enhancement, revised and rethought for a more contemporary use, on the other. Today the park is a new equipped public space for the city, playing an important role as a link between the monumental area and the historic centre, offering new services and functions that can be experienced at all hours of the day and night in complete safety. The central element of the park is a large open meadow and is punctuated along its two longest edges by circle-shaped lines of plants, creating 'rooms' within which are smaller spaces, equipped according to use. Crowning the short edges of the park are the two multifunctional circular areas, and along the entire perimeter there is a cycle and pedestrian path. The trees and vegetation of the different 'rooms' have been deliberately selected from native and local plants. It comprises a wide variety of trees, hedges, shrubs, rose bushes and a large area dedicated to lawns, which significantly contributes to the improvement of the urban environment, mitigating the heat island, promoting biodiversity, soil permeability and rebalancing the relationship between shade and exposure to the sun.

Dialogue with the team

Emanuele Bortolotti, Paolo Palmulli, Alessandro Battaglia, Massimo Brignoli, Sara Spiriti, Pierpaolo Tagliola

The Parco Te project is the fruit of complex interdisciplinary work. Expertise from a range of fields has been brought to bear on exploring this historic and protected place and acquiring a good understanding of it, looking at the potential ways in which it could be modernised and turned into a proper contemporary park. How have you intervened in the area of Palazzo Te?

Emanuele From the outset we realised it was necessary to broaden our perspective, deepen our understanding of the place and look at it from different points of view: from the historical to the urban angle and then that of the landscape and nature. Intervening today in an urban fabric of great value and one that, in this case, is on the UNESCO World Heritage list, that of the city of Mantua, requires not just wider and interdisciplinary skills, but also the sensitivity that it takes to bring historical places up to date and make them accessible and usable in the contemporary world. Conserving today signifies revaluing existing landscapes, giving new meaning to them and improving their quality to restore them to the urban fabric and its inhabitants in a contemporary key.

Sara Yes, heritage sites can be reactivated precisely through landscape design without neglecting a contemporary character. Over the years, we have developed an approach based on strategic guidelines, diagrams, and meta-design forms. We have grown this approach by working on various projects in relationship with important monumental pre-existences. These tools have enabled us to discuss the most important principles with all the actors involved, including citizens, to set project guidelines and consolidate a shared imagination. This approach is particularly relevant within very long decision-making processes and realisations, as often happens in heritage intervention and redevelopment projects.

As often happens when you work in listed historical areas or contexts it is also fundamental to come to an agreement with the public administration over the objectives of the project.

Emanuele The project has been carried out in full agreement with the Mantuan local authorities. What we were determined to create right from the start was a living, vital area of parkland: in fact, the motto, the title of Parco Te is: 'The city belongs to those who live in it'. So, there was never any question of treating the project solely as that of a formal park, even one with its roots in history and in the monumental area, but as the design of a living open space, a park to be enjoyed in the daytime and the evening.

How did you put the work team together?

Paolo The team from the studio that worked on the park was assembled from the outset with the aim of giving us more areas of expertise, in order to tackle the project in the most correct way. It was made up of architects, agronomists, town planners and botanists who, by exchanging ideas with one another in this interdisciplinary framework, have given the project a solid grounding and made it capable of increasing in value over time, both in the concept and final design phase, and on the construction site.

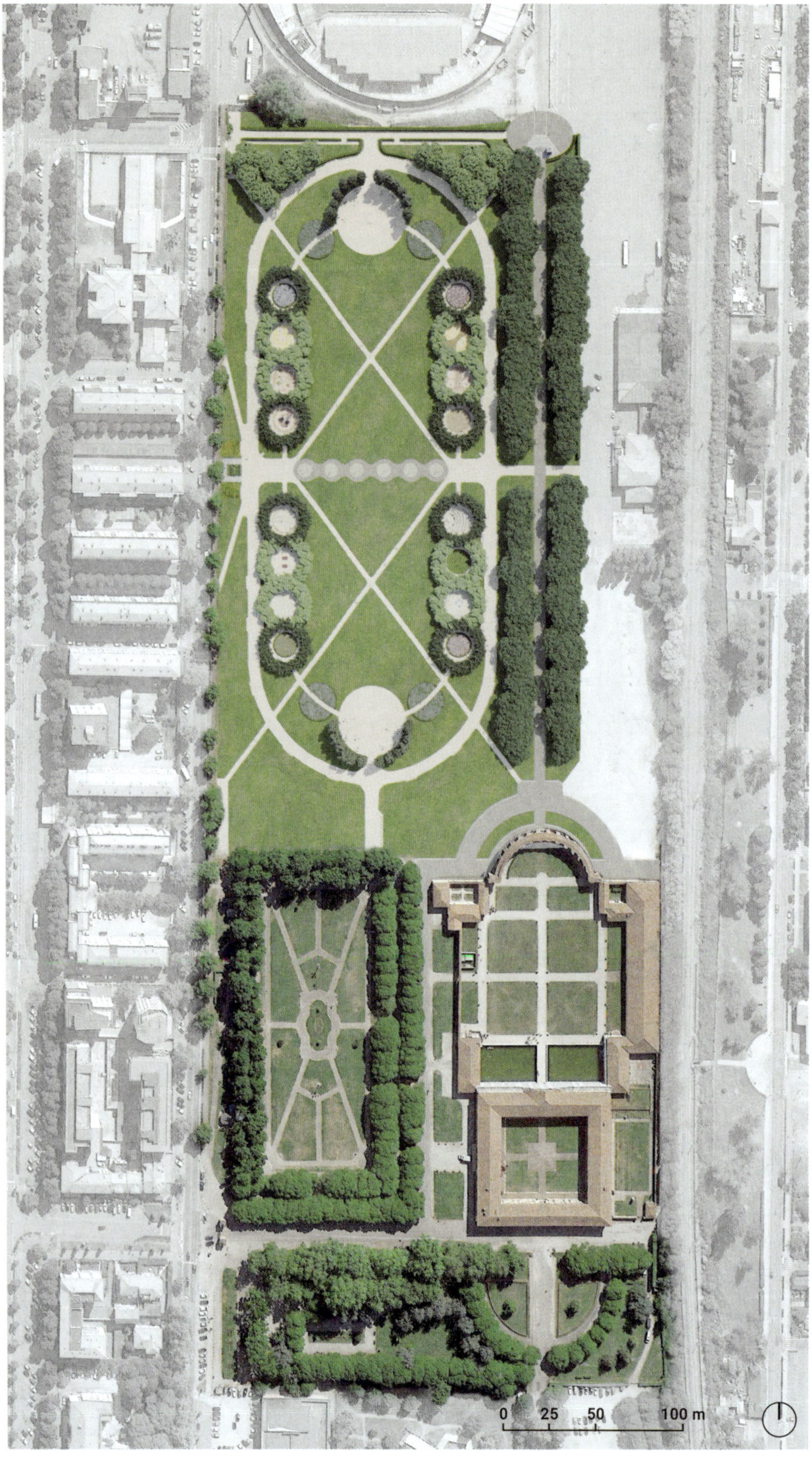

On this page: plan of the park. Facing page and following pages: some photos of the park.

Pierpaolo The team's work was characterised from the start by great internal synergies, as there were different aspects that had to be considered. The project required a degree of formality, being a historical location, but above all because it was linked to a monument like Palazzo Te that presented certain specific forms which we have emphasised and enhanced in our reinterpretation of the place, in part to draw attention to its presence. On the other hand, we had to make some very technical choices, in the face of very difficult ground and the need to find new vegetation capable of surviving in the long term, to integrate the intervention with what already existed and make it sustainable, and at the same time respond to the formal necessities of the project.

Alessandro The construction site experience was also carried out in the spirit of dialogue and discussion with all those involved. When technicians and workers work in synergy with each other, great enthusiasm is generated, which also makes it possible to realise the project in the best possible way, quickly and efficiently, and to feel the energy that everyone brings to a project, in this case Parco Te, which is so important for the city and its citizens. This is an aspect that is sometimes given little attention, but which has its own great value.

So, you started with an in-depth study of the place's historical roots?

Massimo Yes. The first step was to carry out a thorough study of the area. The park of Palazzo Te is a place of inestimable value, one of the most important UNESCO sites in Italy, that holds a direct dialogue with the fabric of the contemporary city, in which it is in fact located today. The project of the park is positioned in this dialogue between history and the present day. A history that for us has been an important reference. We have uncovered a true palimpsest of the many layers of transformation that this place has undergone over time, looking for signs that could still have significance for the contemporary city. So, we have treated the memory of the place not as a static element, but as a dynamic one, still capable of reinventing itself today.

The park used to be located on an island, and Mantua was a city entirely surrounded by water.

Massimo In the time of the Gonzaga duchy (from 1300 to 1700), Palazzo Te was located on the Isola del Te, in the so-called Lago del Paiolo that surrounded the city of Mantua, so that it too was bounded by water. It was one of the most famous delizie (suburban residences) of the late Renaissance, designed by Giulio Romano, and on the island, which was obviously private, there were gardens, farmland, nurseries, hunting grounds and places of entertainment. During that period, the park was already opened to the common people at certain moments. When the Gonzagas, during the 18th century, lost the duchy first to the Austrians and then to Napoleonic rule, the park was given a new layout and the role of a public promenade, and the forms of the park were renewed as well. For instance, circles appeared, as formal elements. The circle is a shape that recurs often in Mantuan culture, and it is one of those that we wanted to echo.

In a way the project underlines not just the presence of Palazzo Te, but also that of other historical structures in the area.

Massimo Yes. Another operation we carried out in the phase of study and analysis was to mark the different important monumental nodes, or centres, that are dotted around the area, and we tried through a system of linkages/connecting routes to reconstruct a hinge between the existing city and those monumental elements. In this way we rediscovered the value of some pre-existing features, such as the Palazzina Liberty, previously in a rather out-of-the-way position, and the Piazza delle Aquile on the north side.

Where exactly have you intervened in the area of Palazzo Te?

Paolo The part in which we intervened the most is the former racecourse: a large green 'room' which we have left as an open space. Bounded by large groups of trees, the area was underutilised and greatly or excessively exposed to the sun. Up until a short time ago it housed football pitches, and so could not be used much by the people of the city at any time of the year.

How were the spaces of the project configured?

Emanuele Inside the great central green room of the old racecourse we proposed planting a system of trees of lower height and grouped in circles, re-proposing the subdivision between a larger room and smaller ones. In addition, we took up and underlined the central axis that leads from the historic city straight to the Palazzina Liberty, along which a fountain has been located, evoking the presence of the water in the area in the past and in a way creating an element of play for the park as well. Two large green exedras with pyramidal oaks close the grand central vista, just like in the courtyard of Palazzo Te. From the city, in addition to the central axis, run two other axes, one in the direction of the exedra of Palazzo Te, deliberately framed by a careful calibration of the masses of vegetation to make the most of its presence through well-defined vistas. The central avenue running from the historical Porta delle Aquile has been reconfigured as one of the main routes of access.

For each of these smaller rooms you went on to define a programme of functions that allow the park to be used in different ways all through the day.

Emanuele Yes, we have defined the contents of the park, its functions, by its users, their age brackets, and different interests, exploiting the space of the twelve green rooms present in the project. The green rooms are circles of about twenty metres in diameter, in each of which we have set a different activity. The route that runs in a ring all the way round the edge of the park has been conceived as a cycle and foot path illuminated in the daytime and under CCTV surveillance at night. We have also added a level of smart use of the park: through the locally accessible and free wi-fi connection people can access an app which they can use to discover the various activities and the programmes of events held in the different spaces.

The choice of vegetation is the result of an in-depth study that led to the selection of indigenous plants, to ensure the park's greater resilience over time.

Pierpaolo The prime factor in achieving resilience in a public park and ensuring its low maintenance cost is the correct choice of plants, to suit the soil, the local environment, and the climatological data of the area. We also selected plants based on their longevity and their form, to restore a lasting, wide-ranging place. Form was of great importance to follow the architectural lines of the project and the context, then make the appropriate technical choices related to the characteristics of the ground. For this reason, the trees and other vegetation planted in the various rooms have been drawn directly from the range of native and local plants.

Emanuele This is an area in which there are many plant nurseries, and the vegetation chosen will serve to complement and enrich the variety of plants already present in the park, improving the urban environment, mitigating the heat island effect, favouring biodiversity and the permeability of the soil, and re-establishing the balance between shade and exposure to the sun.

Top: glimpses at dusk of the paths and circles of trees around the perimeter of the park.

Top: one of the park's tree circles at a busy moment.

On the following pages: general views of the park, and of the pre-existing stadium.

History as a landscape legacy for the future

Conversation with

Mattia Palazzi
Mayor of the municipality of Mantua

In recent years Mantua has staked a great deal on the quality and role of its public spaces in terms of accessibility and cultural activities, as an added value that frames the historical and monumental heritage of the city, holding a dialogue with it. What strategies, visions and actions have you taken and are still taking in your work on the city's system of public spaces?

In 2016 Mantua was the first city to be made Italian Capital of Culture. This gave a powerful incentive both considering the promotion of the city and cultural production. Since that time, we have made major investments to ensure that the initial momentum did not peter out over the following years. We have never stopped investing in culture, focusing on originality and strong ties with our history and our historical and monumental heritage, a clear mark of our identity. In line with this vision, we have chosen to upgrade and enhance many of our monuments, historic buildings and public spaces, such as the Palazzo della Ragione and Palazzo del Podestà, damaged in the earthquake of 2012, the beautiful Piazza Leon Battista Alberti and the Torre della Gabbia, from which it will shortly become possible again, after hundreds of years, to enjoy a particularly evocative panorama. We have invested in our museums, from Palazzo San Sebastiano, which now houses the MACA, the Museo delle Collezioni Antiche, to Palazzo Te, which is today offering a rich set of proposals of great value on a national and international level, in part thanks to the activity of the Fondazione Palazzo Te.

With the world of culture and entertainment we have staged numerous events, performances and festivals that have turned our historic centre into a place that is not just beautiful and welcoming but also filled with activities.

How does the Parco Te project fit into the city's policies with regard to public space?

In this context Parco Te assumes a twofold significance. On the one hand, it is a green lung, a space for life, activity and socialisation restored to all the people of Mantua. On the other, it is one of the key elements of an operation of reconnection of the city's districts with the historic centre that has been underway for years. The project of regeneration of this area of the city had been begging for and deserving attention for too long.

Today it is part of a programme of public works that envisages the upgrading of roads and pavements, cycle and pedestrian underpasses, bike routes and parks, as well of course as the reclamation and renewal of the whole of the area surrounding the park as far as Palazzo Te.

Intervening in a historic location like the area around Palazzo Te, a UNESCO World Heritage Site, with the main objective of making the park more relevant, liveable, usable, and accessible for all the city's inhabitants, in constant dialogue with all the public players involved, is a courageous and visionary undertaking. What have been the biggest challenges you have faced?

The main challenge was to come up with a project that was in perfect harmony and continuity with the history of the place, with the presence of one of the most beautiful buildings in the world and with the feelings of the city's population, fruit of a collective and individual historical relationship of great emotional intensity handed down from generation to generation. This has stimulated a wide-ranging public debate out of which many ideas and visions have emerged, and which have sometimes led to us making modifications to the project.

In brief, the challenge has been to create a park that was not just 'for' the city but 'of' the city. This is why, in 2020, using our own resources, we staged a competition and then entrusted the design to AG&P greenscape. After a thorough study and exchange of ideas, we were able to draw up the definitive project and hold a public tender for the executive planning and realisation of the works, awarded to a temporary grouping of contractors made up of Tea Reteluce, Reggiani Srl and Bottoli Costruzioni, represented by Mantova Ambiente, and the subsequent selection of the AG&P greenscape practice as a partner for the definitive architectural design of the Parco Te.

There have been many protagonists of this challenge, and among them a fundamental part has been played by the Ministry of Culture, which has funded the project in its entirety as part of the Piano Strategico – Grandi Progetti Beni Culturali 2020-21-22, with an investment of 5.2 million euros.

The second challenge has been to stick to a highly complicated time schedule in a period characterised by marked increases in the cost of materials and the time required to obtain them, resulting in slowdowns in the execution of works at a national level. Nevertheless, the deadlines were met, and the park was opened at the end of August 2023.

The Parco Te also represents a possible model of how to intervene in the historical heritage, improving its quality and bringing its uses up to date. What are the most interesting aspects developed in the Parco Te project that serve as examples for similar interventions?

Certainly, one of the most significant aspects has been the one linked to use. Every aspect of the park, including the aesthetic ones, has been considered in relation to the people who are going to live those spaces. So, it is not a solely aesthetic, spectacular, aspect that has been placed at the centre, but one intended to be popular and to ensure the quality of the experience offered. We could say that the two basic ingredients have been beauty and functionality, in a relationship of continual exchange between everyday life and coherence with the past, arriving at a final solution that combines the response to a need of the present, linked to the necessity for spaces that can be used serenely and safely, with the enhancement and adaptation to today's needs of a historical, artistic and symbolic heritage of exceptional value. And then, of course, there's the environmental theme. Eighty thousand square metres of open spaces signify well-being, sustainability and contact with nature. The trees of the Parco Te help to lower the emission of carbon dioxide in the air and add to the roughly 40,000 trees that are already present in the city, in public parks and gardens and in forested and natural areas.

I believe that today's cities, and not just Mantua, need to re-forge ties, to recover quality of life, so that 'residing' becomes more and more a question of 'inhabiting' and 'inhabiting' more and more one of 'sharing'. There is a 'fossilised' way of looking at history and its vestiges, as if at a photograph of an instant in the past. But there was a time in which what we now consider historical was an everyday experience, consistent with its own era and able to respond to the needs and desires of that time. I believe Parco Te is a tangible example of how it is possible to marry respect for the value of history with daily life, of how the experience of beauty can coexist with the experience of the useful, nourishing each other. This is Parco Te, an everyday experience, and a new page of an old story.

Care

Caring for nature with a mix of maintenance and environmental education

Nowadays, various types of action are aimed at increasing the areas dedicated to vegetation to improve the urban quality of our cities, where possible and with all available means. These may take the form of regeneration projects of varying size and type, in which nature is increasingly an essential pivot; interventions for the reuse or renovation of buildings, which attempt to make nature an essential and integrated element of the project; urban reforestation programmes and bottom-up actions that bring nature, people and the built environment into dialogue. The centrality of vegetation in the urban fabric has become a fundamental factor in triggering part of that process of change necessary to safeguard the environment and the well-being of the urban fabric and the people who live there.

However, we need to consider that nature is a living element that develops and transforms over time, requiring monitoring, management and maintenance programmes that accompany it practically throughout its entire life cycle. But the issue today is no longer one of just planting as many plants as possible: the goal for the coming years is to integrate into landscape projects also the management and care of the plant heritage already present and that which we are grafting into our cities. This is the purpose in which we need to invest so as to lay the foundations and build a future in the name of environmental quality, biodiversity and people's well-being that can last over time. It is, for example, a less worthwhile effort than one might imagine and a bad example to plant a large number of trees if one does not monitor their rooting, development and does not water the young plants when necessary. If, due to carelessness or technical errors, more than 10 per cent of new plants are lost shortly after their planting, one can reasonably speak of an operation that has turned out poorly, of resources largely squandered. But when this happens, the fact is almost never highlighted because it would detract from the great communicative power that is linked today to this virtuous practice.

Dealing with a subject as dynamic and sensitive as nature, it is essential to know how to manage its enormous vitality and complexity. Plant life has an unexpected potential for growth. There are many plants capable of generating an astonishing increase in biomass very quickly from seed or seedling. The ability of the landscape architect in the design phase, of the implementer in the planting phase and of the maintainer in the post-planting phase, must be harnessed to encourage, support, manage and correctly guide the enormous vital potential of the plant world.

If architecture usually offers the maximum of its beauty as soon as it is created and then inexorably ages, albeit at different rates, a vegetation-based work, once created, will begin a process of progressive evolution up to the maximum level of maturity and beauty, and then follow an ageing cycle that, if followed well, can continue for a very long time.

But it is not only the post-planting maintenance that is the critical element that will influence the result of any initiative: a poorly designed green space, created with the wrong methods, with poor plant material or unsuitable for the site, in the presence of poor soil quality or difficult climatic conditions, tends not to develop as expected, and without adequate maintenance it will decay very quickly until it becomes wild and disappears.

The conditions under which the plant will be set are never sufficiently taken into account. On the contrary, the costs of implementing landscape projects, and especially those relating to the quality of the plant material and soil in which the plants will be planted, along with the maintenance are always the first to be cut and underestimated. Poor consideration of these factors has an even more negative impact when operating in environments, such as urban areas, in which existing conditions prove to be particularly limiting and unfavourable for the development of greenery.

It is very difficult to communicate effectively to operators, administrators, but also to end users how a well-executed landscape design, suitable living conditions for plants and adequate maintenance, over time, are not only fundamental elements for their future but an excellent investment for administrations, as this generates an increase in urban and environmental quality, an enhancement of the asset and an improvement in the quality of life for all citizens. Moreover, the costs related to the above will be largely compensated for by the enhancement and increased commercial appeal for the private operator and investor as well. Saving on the quality and maintenance of greenery is a resounding own goal at all levels.

Taking care of plants and trees, however, does not only mean providing an adequate level of maintenance. Caring for nature is a process that begins before the plants are put in the ground, in creating all the necessary conditions for their subsequent life and development.

And it is from the bottom, particularly from the soil, that satisfactory development and the quality of future vegetation will originate. There are factors that are never talked about but which are absolutely decisive for the desired results when creating a new space for nature. In many projects and interventions, the study of the soil where plants will be set, how the plants will adapt to different soils and climatic conditions, what the planting methods will be, and what care and irrigation support will be provided after planting, are neglected. The result is that where these aspects are not taken care of, most trees and plants do not survive the transplanting process or grow stunted and in the best of cases may halt development and growth.

In particular, knowing the characteristics of the soil is the first step towards ensuring the life and development of plants and limiting disease. Moreover, soil is rich when it con-

On the previous page: a view of BAM – Biblioteca degli Alberi Milano. On this page: a view of the Siemens park and entertainment for employees and their families.

tains a good amount of organic substance, a condition that makes it a precious container of plant and animal biodiversity through an intricate web of relationships between solid particles, microorganisms, animals that live in the soil, chemical elements, air and water. It is therefore safe to say that, generally speaking, soil improvement is just as topical and urgent an issue as the need to increase plant biodiversity and plant lots of trees. It is worth mentioning the huge extent of poor or impoverished soils caused by building and industrial developments or by agricultural monocultures, and the soils contaminated by waste, and often illegal dumps. Then there are the soils compacted by heavy vehicles, which are asphyxiating for plants because they are covered by impermeable or almost impermeable pavements due to waterlogging, and soils impoverished by landslides or by increased drought and surface aridity.

Another often underestimated issue that has a very negative impact on the process of enhancing and renaturing sites is that of the poor ecological and environmental sensitivity of a large part of the population, especially in urban centres: estrangement from the natural world despite an absolute need for it, poor respect for urban nature, which often translates into vandalism, are very common phenomena that are little reduced even in the presence of environmental and climatic emergencies. Furthermore, in urban environments the anthropogenic load in relation to the scarcity of public green spaces is a factor that must always be taken into account because it makes maintenance more onerous.

Until people accept nature as a friend, respect it and defend it as an indispensable ally, it will be difficult to see processes of real and lasting transformation of the environment around us. From this point of view, we believe that only the involvement and environmental education of end users, from an early age, in families, schools and neighbourhoods, to teach them to make a more conscious and careful use of landscape spaces, can profoundly change the current scenario.

Consideration of the landscape as heritage, and the dissemination of a greater knowledge of nature and its transformation processes are the prerequisites to make people more aware of the value of the places they live in, more open to other places and cultures, and more responsible with regard to landscape management and care.

Thanks to its know-how and long-standing design practice, AG&P greenscape is particularly aware of these issues and considers environmental education from an early age to be a fundamental factor for the necessary change of scenario. Indeed, for some time it has been promoting environmental education through courses, publications and the organisation of events for adults, young people and children, not only in participatory design experiences, but in direct and assisted involvement in public events during the creation of new gardens and urban parks (during sowing, planting, harvesting, and direct maintenance), or in guided tours with in-depth botanical studies. For this reason, the firm has also been commissioned to supervise the maintenance of the landscape projects it carries out and to organise in-depth botanical events for the public. The activities carried out in the BAM park illustrated in the book are an eloquent example of this commitment.

On this page: a glimpse of BAM – Biblioteca degli Alberi Milano.

UniCredit

Causa Pia d'Adda kindergarten, Segrate

The project for the kindergarten park proposes a comfortable, varied, and multi-functional open space to allow the children to find new stimuli in contact with nature and natural elements, with changing landscapes at every change of season: not only a space for playing, but also an opportunity for outdoor education and cultivating environmental awareness.

BAM – Biblioteca degli Alberi Milano

Parco BAM (Biblioteca degli Alberi Milano), designed by Petra Blaisse's Amsterdam-based firm Inside/Outside, is located inside the Porta Nuova area, a major urban regeneration project of several disused areas, whose showpiece is this public park, run in a public-private partnership by the Fondazione Riccardo Catella. The history of AG&P greenscape and BAM have been closely linked ever since the realisation of the new park, which in a very short space of time has succeeded in becoming a crucial part of the city. The practice was initially responsible for management of work on the entire project, launching at the same time cultural initiatives to involve local citizens in the various stages of the layout of the park and getting them to play a part in the transformation underway. Later on, the practice supported the Fondazione Riccardo Catella all the way through the period immediately following the creation of BAM, assisting it in all aspects regarding the botanical side of the project, from maintenance to cultural activities, becoming Botanical Content Partner of BAM in 2020. Responsible not only for the maintenance of the park, but also for the staging of a number of events open to the public during the year, such as the 'Nature Talk' and the 'Botanical Tour', AG&P greenscape has focused in particular on producing the content of the column 'La botanica di BAM', carried on the park's website and its profiles on social networks. Alongside images of the plants in the park, selected for the column, can be found brief accounts, detailed studies, and anecdotes, aimed at getting people to know the place better and to feel themselves part of it, developing a sense of belonging and care.

Dialogue with the team

Emanuele Bortolotti, Paolo Palmulli, Pierpaolo Tagliola, Mariagiusi Troisi

Unlike architecture, nature is a living object, which changes over time, and therefore needs constant and continuous care. AG&P greenscape directly followed the Works Management for the realisation of the Biblioteca degli Alberi (Library of Trees) in Milan. What was it like to work on such a structured project?

Paolo The Biblioteca degli Alberi is a botanical park, with many areas, whose variety of spaces and vegetation are what makes it stand out. This complexity was already addressed on site with almost monothematic specialists, coordinated by a single figure to hold all the specificities together, following the interdisciplinary methodological approach that our studio has developed over time. Moreover, from the earliest stages of construction, the park has always been a place of dialogue and experimentation for us, carried out in close contact with all the local workers. In our decades of experience working in the field, we have learnt to listen to and discuss with every professional involved, to be able to make decisions in a very short time.

Once the park was completed, how did the task of supervising maintenance activities and narrating the botany of the park come about?

Emanuele As Paolo mentioned, BAM is a park rich in vegetation and with a variety of areas. It has more than 500 trees, belonging to 100 species, and more than 135,000 plants, including herbs, aquatic plants, bulbs, hedges, shrubs, and creepers. Maintenance is essential for its proper functioning. This was very clear to everyone, right from the early stages of the project. For this reason, Fondazione Riccardo Catella, having taken over the management of the park with an agreement signed directly with the Milan City Council, appointed us to be BAM's Botanical Content Partner, to oversee the design and supervision of maintenance activities and the botany of the park.

Isn't it unusual for a public park to provide maintenance supervision?

Paolo The maintenance supervision assignment we have been given is not a common practice; far from it. However, there is a premise to be made: the maintenance cost parameters of public projects are interpreted in an outdated way. Today, among these parameters, we can no longer disregard evaluating the amount of well-being per capita that a park offers to the citizens who can use it. We always think of maintenance as a one-off cost, without considering that it is instead part of an investment for the future, one of the fundamental aspects of managing an open space, to guarantee a constant quality of landscape projects, without which it becomes difficult to truly take care not only of the city, but of all its citizens.

Emanuele It is a matter of understanding caring for a place in a dialectical way, centred on a system of common reference values, with the precise intention of building a place that is open, inclusive and that places the community of people who use and pass through it at the centre. Because of this approach, maintenance supervision is integrated with the story of the botany of the park, both of which work, also and above all, in synergy with each other.

How do the two aspects of your job as BAM Botanical Content Partner, that of supervising maintenance and the storytelling you do about the park, work together?

Mariagiusi These two activities are very closely linked. As Emanuele said, in a way, one supports the other. The storytelling of the botany of the park and the related activities of meetings and walks are how we have made people aware of the nature of BAM and the great maintenance and care it requires. If you make people aware of how a park should be treated, maintenance also becomes easier. It is a kind of outreach programme, but also environmental education.

Were people involved from the very beginning in the different phases of the park's realisation?

Paolo Yes, of course. From the earliest stages of the construction site, open moments were organised involving the citizens through various entertainment activities, to make them participate and be more aware of the park's creation. Once the park was inaugurated, it was immediately clear that this relationship with the people could and should be a positive aspect to be promoted.

However, it is necessary to understand that although it is a public park, BAM was designed from the beginning with much higher standards, which require equally high care and maintenance.

Emanuele A real maintenance project starts well before the park is finished. Already in the building site phases it is necessary to take into account certain fundamental aspects, such as creating the best possible conditions for the life and subsequent development of the vegetation, through a number of specific actions: from choosing the most suitable plants for the site, and the correct period in which they will be planted; positioning trees and shrubs at the correct distance; checking and improving the richness of the soil and its permeability, as well as the quality of the plants themselves – the plants must be healthy and well formed; to checking and calibrating the irrigation systems.

By preparing everything meticulously, maintenance can be facilitated. As with every project, this is divided into ordinary and extraordinary and involves following the overall evolution of the space created. In a park as complex as BAM, it is a question of being able to hold together the vision of the overall project, to intervene in timely fashion where necessary, without losing sight of the complexity of the site and finding solutions adapted to each situation.

The park has been used from the very beginning by citizens and is now felt as part of the everyday space by those who use it or walk through it.

Pierpaolo Yes, it has to all intents and purposes become a real attraction for the whole city. However, the citizens who use the park represent both a strength and a difficulty.
A strength because it is an active and integrated place with its content and more. A weakness, because the park's great attraction leads to large numbers of people commensurate with the size of the spaces and especially the lawns, and it is often difficult to manage the load. Above all, it requires very careful maintenance and sometimes even the rebuilding of some of its parts.

Mariagiusi Sometimes we also have to solve unforeseen problems or have to adapt some of the park's solutions to the dynamics that citizens have established with this place over time. For this reason, it is interesting that the two areas we work on, maintenance and botanical storytelling, then meet in aspects of this kind: telling people not to trample on the lawns because they are growing, becomes an essential part of maintenance.

Indeed, adapting new functions is also essential. A park is an open place, whether public or private, and the use people make of it can also be unexpected and require adjustments.

Pierpaolo Absolutely. One example that comes to mind is the creation of the blooming room.

On previous pages, large photo, and top: views of the park; below: aerial view on the blooming room.

On this page, top: a glimpse of the swing area; right: a detail of the park pond.

On the next page: aerial photo of the park.

The blooming lawns are so beautiful that people used to come in and without realising often created damage. It was a big problem to manage. We responded in a proactive manner, without raising barriers, by trying to accommodate this request, and created a walkable ring within the central flower meadow to give people the opportunity to enter and enjoy the spectacle more closely. It is important that people understand that caring also means respecting and paying attention to the environment around us. Environmental education is a long process, but we strongly believe in it.

Speaking of which, I am proud to mention that this park gained a recognition in the Urban Regeneration and Public Spaces category of the Dubai International Award for Sustainable Development, an initiative sponsored by the United Nations to recognise projects that have a major positive impact on improving their environment.

Mariagiusi During the Covid lockdown, BAM was also treated as a palimpsest to communicate with people locked in their homes. We used the lawns to produce writings and compose messages, as a moment of solidarity with people. And when distancing was later imposed on us, we had circles made on the lawns to show people the areas where they could stay. There are so many aspects that we can consider 'care', and the studio tries to decline each tool according to what the needs or requirements of the moment may be.

Have other assignments of this kind followed?

Pierpaolo BAM was a pilot project for us. However, in recent times, AG&P has often been entrusted with design management and maintenance supervision (as, for example, in the project carried out for Gucci). With a few years of experience behind us, we can say that supervising maintenance, as the first step in taking care of a park, can make a big difference: nature is a living element that evolves. It is never something finished, and there is a constant continuity in its growth and transformation; being able to guide the maintainer and follow these changes step by step brings better results for everyone, for us designers, for the client and for those who use parks and gardens.

How has the botanical section changed over time?

Mariagiusi Initially, the botanical section offered content that also dealt with maintenance, each accompanied by its own photographs. Over time, however, the focus has shifted to purely botanical aspects only. By now the park, in terms of structure and organisation, is known to everyone, and there was a risk of becoming repetitive over time by recounting the themes of maintenance supervision. So, we were happy to focus on the botanical story. Moreover, in recent years we have been working more on social networking topics, as well as the park's website. This is a way of being closer to citizens, especially young people, and to pass on to them some knowledge about the park, to promote its care and respect for nature.

LANO

Environmental education

Environmental education is one of the most important knowledge tools that can be used to bring people closer to the landscape, especially when a new park comes to life. AG&P greenscape's role as Botanical Content Partner is functional in transmitting knowledge of the park to citizens, in all its aspects, including those dedicated to maintenance. Cultural programmes, moments of exchange and debate, and guided tours are important opportunities to involve people and make them more aware of the value of nature, of the care it necessarily requires as it transforms over time, and of how much each of us can contribute every day to improving the condition of the urban landscape in which we live, in a reciprocal exchange of well-being.

KASK

Acer

The Biblioteca degli Alberi: taking care of a public space

Conversation with

Francesca Colombo
Director of BAM – Biblioteca degli Alberi Milano

Taking care of a public space, today, is something that is of potentially very great value. How has the plan for 'taking care' of BAM been conceived?

It has its roots in the Fondazione Riccardo Catella's extensive experience in urban development and the optimisation of public spaces, in a study of international best practices and in the creation of a sustainable business model and a system of public/private governance that became a reality on 5 July 2019 with the signing of the partnership agreement between COIMA, the Fondazione Riccardo Catella and the municipality of Milan for the management of the Biblioteca degli Alberi public park in Milan. We feel strongly our responsibility to *take care* of a public good. We have worked on creating a set of benchmarks, an inclusive, open identity that places the community to which this place belongs at the centre, an innovative operating model and a managerial strategy that extends the concept of *taking care* to all aspects of this place's life.

Taking care for us means a day-to-day commitment to ensuring the space is clean, well maintained and equipped and ready to welcome safely all the diverse communities that make use of the park: from children, sportsmen and women, the elderly, and workers to tourists. In the park there are playgrounds, as well as areas with fitness equipment, seating and free wi-fi. But the most interesting part of the project is the vision of the concept of *care* in terms of making the most of the place through culture. The BAM project is first of all a cultural and educational project, which sets out to speak to its communities through the language of the arts in order to achieve the objective of promoting the culture of environmental sustainability. Since 2019, we have staged more than 1,050 cultural and educational events for the city's residents free of charge, stimulating over 129,000 people with experiences able to stir emotions and arouse a sense of wonder, curiosity and belonging.

How has the cultural and educational programme been developed?

The cultural and educational programme has been conceived and run entirely under my oversight, together with a professional team of 10 people we have selected and that handles every detail of the programming, from production to communication, to fundraising, and renders the programme unique and site-specific. A modern-day agora.

The cultural programme, along with the many projects that we have come up with to stimulate people's active participation (Radici project, BAMFriends, numerous projects in collaboration with universities, the voluntary work scheme, etc.), has made BAM an important resource for the cultural and social development of the area. BAM is a cultural player in the city, able to network with over 168 cultural entities ranging from those based in the city to international bodies!

And finally, for us *taking care* means that BAM can make a social, cultural, and environmental impact on the local area. The numbers and goals achieved so far reassure us and help us to see that we are heading in the right direction.

The pilot project of public/private collaboration with which the BAM park is run is a prospect that needs to be tested and developed. In what aspects do you think that it is a good model and in what ways could it be improved?

The course taken by the Fondazione Riccardo Catella with the project BAM has made it possible to show clearly the characteristics of this innovative model of management that make it an important means of local development.

In the first place, it permits a dialogue between the objectives of the public and private sectors, bringing different skills and resources to bear on the management of urban parkland, and thus acknowledging it as an element of essential interest to the community. The private sphere is no longer concerned simply with making a profit but, through its activity, has become a producer of social value and well-being for the area and the community to which it belongs.

It allows public functions to take on board the sort of innovation, efficient use of resources and productivity typical of the business sector, and private enterprises to redirect their goals towards a model that takes the social, cultural, and environmental impact of its actions into account.

It favours the establishment of a relationship of trust and collaboration between the various actors in the area, encouraging the formation of a network of companies and institutions, as well as bodies in the not-for-profit sector, that allows them to work synergistically.

All these factors have emerged clearly over the course of the creation of BAM, where we can see that in the space of five years we have succeeded in constructing a virtuous network of partner companies that share the objectives of the park. By choosing to commit themselves to the preservation of urban biodiversity, they have become involved in the joint planning of experiences that speak of sustainability, express shared values, and have an impact on the city.

How can the public/private model implemented for BAM evolve?

BAM is an innovative model in Italy for the cultural management of a public park. We are happy to share our experience and hope to be ‘trailblazers’, and that other cities will follow this model to make our public parks examples of excellence, as has already happened with the privately run ones, effectively promoted by the Grandi Giardini Italiani association to which BAM belongs. It is unquestionably fundamental to go on assessing what we are doing in an objective manner and giving a transparent account of our activity to all the stakeholders in the model. My background in engineering has always led me to assign great importance to figures and to reporting, and I think that this is essential to continuing to improve our work, identifying the parameters of success, and rendering this model of management more and more scalable and applicable even in different contexts. What can be improved and that we hope to achieve is a greater involvement of the private sector, whether we are talking about companies located around BAM, companies that share these values or private citizens who can contribute to the support of the park through small but concrete acts of giving back.

Knowledge is also an important aspect of 'taking care' of a place, all the more so if it is a green space. How have you seen the use that people make of the park change?

Beauty summons beauty, care calls for respect. Through our cultural programme we try to make the park a place for everyone, to get people to understand its nature and to involve them and make them aware of their joint responsibility in taking care of a public park. We strive to maintain a very wide range of plants to enrich urban biodiversity: the park has over 100 botanical species, more than 500 trees that form 22 circular forests and over 135,000 plants, including aromatic herbs, hedges, shrubs, bulbs, creepers, aquatic plants, and weeds.

Many projects have been implemented to exploit this wealth, such as BAM's plant nursery, the numerous workshops for children and adults of the #nature pillar of our cultural programme, botanical and literary walks, guided tours with experienced naturalists and awareness campaigns like that of the adoption of trees, through which people can personalise one of BAM's 500 trees with a plaque and a dedication, and involvement in the Green Community of BAMFriends. All initiatives aimed at establishing a dialogue with an urban garden and learning to respect nature in general. And for the future, there are other projects in the pipeline that will enrich the biodiversity of our urban park.

After five years of work, it's great to see how BAM is gradually leading to the creation of a community that is making use of public space while showing respect for its nature and for the general interest and that wants to play an active part.

BAM's cultural programme plays a fundamental role in guiding the way in which people use and treat this place: where there is beauty and life it is easier to safeguard the public good, and our events help us to create and nurture a strong bond between the people of the city and the park.

Apparatus

Projects credits

The projects in the credits refer to the selection illustrated in the book and are organised in order of appearance.

All projects result from the team collaboration presented on page 271 according to specific competencies.

'Other project partners' refers only to the direct collaborators of AG&P greenscape and not all the companies and figures involved in the project.

The following acronyms in the project credits indicate the services in the landscape field carried out by AG&P greenscape.

MT Master plan
CP Concept
PP Preliminary Design
PD Developed Design
PE Detailed Design
DA Landscape Artistic Supervision
DV Landscape Site Supervision
DG General Site Supervision

1
Nuovo Centroparco
Segrate (Milan) - IT
2018 - 2019
Area: 1,000,000 sqm
Client: Segrate Municipality
Services: MT
Landscape design:
AG&P greenscape

2
Centroparco Lotto 0 and Lotto 1
Segrate (Milan) - IT
2007 - In progress
Area: 250,000 sqm
Client: Iniziative
Services: CP - PP - PD - PE - DG
Landscape design:
AG&P greenscape

3
Centroparco Lotto 5
Segrate (Milan) - IT
2021 - In progress
Area: 85,000 sqm
Client: East Park
Services: CP - PP - PD - PE
Landscape design:
AG&P greenscape

4
Parco del Paleoalveo
Bergamo - IT
2022 - In progress
Area: 86,000 sqm
Client: Ferretti Casa
Services: CP - PP - PD - PE - DV
Landscape design:
AG&P greenscape

5
Crescenzago Park
Milan - IT
2018 - 2023
Area: 14,000 sqm
Client: Europa Risorse
Services: CP - PP - PD - PE - DG
Landscape design:
AG&P greenscape

6
Cascina Merlata Park
Milan - IT
2014 - 2017
Area: 200,000 sqm
Client: Parco Cascina Merlata S.C.A.R.L
Services: PE and technical supervision
Landscape design: PP - PD - DA
by Franco Giorgetta
with Giovanna Longhi

7
Milano 4 You
Segrate (Milan) - IT
2019 - In progress
Area: 300,000 sqm
Client: Sagitta - Sei Oltre
Services: CP - PP - PD - PE - DG
Landscape design:
AG&P greenscape -
MAB Arquitectura
Master plan: MAB Arquitectura

8
Territorial Strategy of the city of Savona
Savona - IT
2023 - 2024
Client: Savona Municipality
Services: Territorial strategy and pre-feasibility projects
Landscape design:
AG&P greenscape
Other project partners:
Mta Associati - Gioia Gibelli -
U-lab - Kcity - Paolo Maneo

9
Waterfront di Levante | Public Areas
Genoa - IT
2021 - In progress
Area: 35,000 sqm
Client: CdS Holding - Starching -
Genoa Municipality
Services: CP - PP - PD - PE - DV
Landscape design:
AG&P greenscape
Master plan:
Renzo Piano Building Workshop
Architectural design:
Renzo Piano Building Workshop -
OBR - Starching

10
Waterfront di Levante | Private Areas
Genoa - IT
2021 - Under construction
Area: 20,000 sqm
Client: Renzo Piano Building Workshop
Services: CP - PP - PD - PE - DA
Landscape design:
AG&P greenscape
Master plan:
Renzo Piano Building Workshop
Architectural design:
Renzo Piano Building Workshop - OBR - Starching

11
Varesina 204 | Certosa District
Milan - IT
2019 - 2023
Area: 3,000 sqm
Client: Real Step Sicaf
Services: CP - PP - PD - PE - DA
Landscape design:
AG&P greenscape
Architectural design:
Giuseppe Tortato Architetti

12
La Forgiatura | Certosa District
Milan - IT
2007 - 2012
Area: 5,000 sqm
Client: Real Step Sicaf
Services: CP - PP - PD - PE - DA
Landscape design:
AG&P greenscape
Architectural design:
Giuseppe Tortato Architetti

13
Giardino Nascosto
Milan - IT
2014 - 2016
Area: 5,000 sqm
Client: Comitato Ponti
Services: CP - PP - PD - DA
Landscape design:
AG&P greenscape

14
Ex Opificio d'Adda
Milan - IT
2009 - 2011
Area: 1,000 sqm
Client: Winter Immobiliare
Services: CP - PP - PD - PE - DA
Landscape design:
AG&P greenscape
Architectural design:
DFA Partners

15
ARIA | Ex Macello
Milan - IT
2021 - In progress
Area: 150,000 sqm
Client: Stantec - Barreca & La Varra - Snøhetta - Mpartner - Redo
Services: PP - PD
Landscape design:
AG&P greenscape - Snøhetta
Architectural design: Snøhetta - Barreca & La Varra - Stantec - CZA Cino Zucchi Architetti - Chapman Taylor Architetti - Mpartner - Fondazione Housing Sociale
Other project partners: Agro Service

16
Office buildings Zona Tortona
Milan - IT
2008
Area: 500 sqm
Client: Private
Services: CP - PP - PD - PE - DA
Landscape design:
AG&P greenscape

17
Parco delle Dune
Genoa - IT
2021 - In progress
Area: 40,000 sqm
Client: Ports of Genoa
Services: CP - PP - PD - DA
Landscape design:
AG&P greenscape

18
Tunnel Subportuale and Parco della Lanterna
Genoa - IT
2022 - In progress
Area: 140,000 sqm
Client: Renzo Piano Building Workshop
Services: CP - PP - PD - PE
Landscape design:
AG&P greenscape
Architectural design: Renzo Piano Building Workshop

19
CityWave
Milan - IT
2020 - Under construction
Area: 17,000 sqm
Client: CityLife
Services: PP - PD - PE - DV
Landscape design:
AG&P greenscape
Architectural design:
Bjarke Ingels Group

20
Largo Treves
Milan - IT
2021 - 2023
Area: 2,000 sqm
Client: V10
Services: CP - PP - PD - PE - DA
Landscape design:
AG&P greenscape

21
Giardini Magolfa-Navigli
Milan - IT
2000 - 2010
Area: 7,000 sqm
Client: Fabrica Immobiliare
Services: CP - PP - PD - PE - DA
Landscape design:
AG&P greenscape

22
Segrate Centro
Segrate (Milan) - IT
2008 - 2010
Area: 5,000 sqm
Client: Centroparco
Services: PP - PD - PE - DA
Landscape design:
AG&P greenscape

23
Parco dei Mulini
Segrate (Milan) - IT
2022 - 2024
Area: 20,000 sqm
Client: Segrate Municipality
Services: CP - PP - PD - PE - DG
Landscape design:
AG&P greenscape

24
Parco della Torre
Milan - IT
2014 - 2018
Area: 20,000 sqm
Client: Lambda - Prelios Integra
Services: CP - PP - PD - PE - DA
Landscape design:
AG&P greenscape

25
New Stadium
Milan - IT
2019
Area: 200,000 sqm
Client: Sportium Progetto CMR
Services: MT (competition finalist)
Landscape design:
AG&P greenscape
Architectural design:
Manica - Sportium Progetto CMR

26
Bosconavigli
Milan - IT
2021 - In progress
Area: 15,000 sqm
Client: Milano 5.0
Services: CP - PP - PD - PE - DA - DV
Landscape design:
AG&P greenscape
Architectural design:
Stefano Boeri Architetti -
Arassociati
Other project partners:
One Shot Real Estate Solutions

27
Giardino delle Scoperte
Segrate (Milan) - IT
2016 - In progress
Area: 15,000 sqm
Client: Iniziative
Services: CP - PP - PD - PE - DA
Landscape design:
AG&P greenscape
Architectural design:
Studio Cocozza

28
Residenze Bergamo+
Bergamo - IT
2013 - 2016
Area: 13,000 sqm
Client: Immobiliare Parco Locatelli
Services: CP - PP - PD - PE - DA
Landscape design:
AG&P greenscape
Architectural design:
ACPV ARCHITECTS
Antonio Citterio Patricia Viel

29
Ex Opificio Magolfa
Milan - IT
2014 - 2018
Area: 800 sqm
Client: Martina Holding
Services: CP - PP - PD - PE - DA
Landscape design:
AG&P greenscape
Architectural design:
DFA Partners

30
Habitaria | Corso Garibaldi 95
Milan - IT
2012 - 2020
Area: 1,200 sqm
Client: Garibaldi 95
Services: CP - PP - PD - PE - DA
Landscape design:
AG&P greenscape
Architectural design: Arassociati

31
Merezzate Smart District
Milan - IT
2016 - 2020
Area: 22,000 sqm
Client: M2P Architetti Associati - Redo
Services: PD
Landscape design:
AG&P greenscape
Master plan: M2P Architetti Associati - UP! Design And Research Lab
Architectural design: MAB Arquitectura - Beretta Associati - Studio Brugellis - Di Franco - Giorgieri

32
Crédit Agricole Green Life
Parma - IT
2017 2019
Area: 70,000 sqm
Client: Crédit Agricole Group Solutions
Services: CP - PP - PD - PE - DA
Landscape design:
AG&P greenscape
Architectural design:
Frigerio Design Group

33
Gucci Hub
Milan - IT
2016 - 2018
Area: 2,400 sqm
Client: Guccio Gucci
Services: CP - PP - PD - PE - DA
Landscape design:
AG&P greenscape
Architectural design: Piuarch

34
HQ Siemens Italia
Milan - IT
2016 - 2019
Area: 25,000 sqm
Client: Siemens
Services: CP - PP - PD - PE - DA
Landscape design:
AG&P greenscape

35
HQ Allianz Italia
Milan - IT
2018 - 2019
Area: 700 sqm
Client: Allianz
Services: CP - PP - PD - PE - DA
Landscape design:
AG&P greenscape
Architectural design:
Arata Isozaki & Associates

36
HQ Fondazione Compagnia di San Paolo | Pocket Campus Bernini
Turin - IT
2020 - 2023
Area: 4,000 sqm
Client: Fondazione Compagnia di San Paolo
Services: CP - PP - PD - PE - DG
Landscape design:
AG&P greenscape
Other project partners:
GAe Engineering

37
Monte Rosa 91
Milan - IT
2020 - 2024
Area: 10,000 sqm
Client: AXA Investment
Services: CP - PP - PD - PE - DA - DV
Landscape design:
AG&P greenscape
Architectural design:
Renzo Piano Building Workshop

38
Parco Te
Mantua - IT
2019 - 2023
Area: 80,000 sqm
Client: Mantua Municipality
Services: CP - PP - PD - DV
Landscape design:
AG&P greenscape

39
Palazzo Citterio | Pinacoteca di Brera
Milan - IT
2021 - In progress
Area: 3,000 sqm
Client: Pinacoteca di Brera
Services: CP - PP - PD - PE - DG
Landscape design:
AG&P greenscape

40
Villa Rezzola
Lerici (La Spezia) - IT
2022 - Under construction
Area: 16,000 sqm
Client: FAI - Fondo Ambiente Italiano
Services: CP - PP - PD - PE - DLV
Landscape design:
AG&P greenscape
Architectural design:
Arch. Roberto Segattini
Other project partners:
Agro Service

41
Zacchera Hotels
Lago Maggiore - IT
2007 - In progress
Area: 30,000 sqm
Client: Zacchera Hotels
Services: CP - PP - PD - PE - DA
Landscape design:
AG&P greenscape

42
Parco del Priamar
Savona - IT
2022 - 2023
Area: 95,000 sqm
Client: Savona Municipality
Services: MT - CP
Landscape design:
AG&P greenscape

43
Rinnovata Pizzigoni School
Milan - IT
2021 - In progress
Area: 17,000 sqm
Client: CityLife
Services: CP - PP - PD - PE
Landscape design:
AG&P greenscape
Architectural design:
Studio Berlucchi

44
BAM – Parco Biblioteca degli Alberi Milano
Milan - IT
2017 - 2018
Area: 80,000 sqm
Client: IN.G.RE Scrl - COIMA
Services: DV - Maintenance supervisoring - Botanical Partner
Landscape design: Inside Outside | Petra Blaisse
Other project partners: Studio Ing. Ceruti, GAe Engineering

45
Causa Pia d'Adda kindergarten
Segrate (Milan) - IT
2007 - 2009
Area: 4,000 sqm
Client: Fondazione Causa Pia d'Adda
Services: CP - PP - PD - PE - DA
Landscape design:
AG&P greenscape
Architectural design:
Studio Cocozza

AG&P greenscape

With forty years of experience, AG&P greenscape is a multidisciplinary landscape laboratory working in the fields of master planning, urban landscape, and garden design. Through all the services of landscape architecture, the studio offers tailor-made solutions, realised with the same passion and craftsmanship on both small and large scale, putting people and their needs at the centre. The aim is to dissolve the boundaries between landscape, architecture, technology, culture, and ecology through a rigorous and careful process of investigation, design, and realisation, to create quality built and natural environments. This multidisciplinary and multi-scalar approach distinguishes the work of the studio, allowing it to be always up-to-date and capable of integrating the challenges of the contemporary city and new landscapes into its design processes. United by a vision that explores the relationship between man and nature at all scales of the project, partners Emanuele Bortolotti and Paolo Palmulli coordinate, together with associate Alessandro Frigerio, a team of over forty professionals including landscape architects, architects, agronomists, urban planners, and naturalists, who make up the creative, technical, and interdisciplinary heart of the studio.

Left: Paolo Palmulli and Emanuele Bortolotti, Partner and Founding Partner of AG&P greenscape.

AG&P greenscape team

Alessandro Battaglia
Architect
Chiara Battini
Architect
Andrea Bortolotti
Tender Specialist
Emanuele Bortolotti
Agronomist and Garden Designer
Francesco Bossola
Architect
Massimo Brignoli
Architect and Urban Designer PhD
Burcin Candan
Landscape Architect
Valeria Carnevali
Communications Manager
Ilaria Chiodini
Office Secretary Assistant
Luca Ciliani
Landscape Architect
Marco Concina
Agro-technician
Ludovica De Ruvo
Agronomist
Sofya Dolgaya
Architect
Chiara Dosso
Landscape Architect
Giorgia Fiorentini
Architect
Barbara Frangi
Landscape Specialist
Alessandro Frigerio
Architect and Urban Designer PhD
Francesca Garzilli
Architect PhD
Federico Ghezzi
Architect
Giulia Gigantino
Architect
Irene Grieco
Architect
Lorenzo Guida
Designer
Georgia Karsioti
Architect
Paolo Maneo
Urban Planner
Igino Marchesin
Graphic and
3D Renderist
Barbara Mariani
Architect
Patrizia Muner
Administrative Manager
Lucia Nadalin
Architect
Kamila Nasretdinova
Landscape Architect
Marco Nelli
Landscape Architect
Andrea Occhetti
Architect and
Landscape Architect
Paolo Palmulli
Architect and Urban Landscape
Specialist
Angelo Parigi
Naturalist and Agro-technician
Michele Pasculli
Landscape Architect
Chiara Peluso
Office Secretary
Marina Polets
Architect
Silvia Puppin
Architect
Edoardo Rebay
Architect
Aldo Rossi
Architect and Urban Designer
Sara Spiriti
Architect
Pierpaolo Tagliola
Agronomist and
Landscape Architect
Mariagiusi Troisi
Environmental Architect
Virginia Vecchi
Urban Planner
Stefania Zavarise
Architect

Authors' biographies

Emanuele Bortolotti
A lifelong enthusiast of nature and the urban landscape, he graduated in science, specialised in garden architecture, and became an AIAPP member. He was one of the founders in 1985 of the AG&P greenscape studio, of which he is now owner together with Paolo Palmulli. In recent years he has overseen works such as Parco Te in Mantua, Bosconavigli in Milan with Stefano Boeri and Arassociati, the award-winning headquarters of Crédit Agricole Italia in Parma. He was the first Italian designer to win a medal at the international competition of the Chelsea Flower Show in London. A lecturer in various specialist courses, he is the author of the book *Il giardino inaspettato,* published by Electa.

Paolo Palmulli
Architect specialised in urban landscape architecture, with experience both in Italy and abroad, partner of AG&P greenscape and member of AIAPP. His most recent projects include the master plan for the Nuovo Centroparco in Segrate, the Waterfront di Levante in Genoa with Renzo Piano and OBR, City-Wave for the BIG studio in Milan CityLife. Co-author of the book *Paesaggio diffuso: l'esperienza di un nuovo quartiere a Segrate* published by Electa. Author of articles for various periodicals in the field, he has collaborated with the Faculty of Architecture of the Politecnico di Milano, with supplementary modules in the Urban Design Workshops and for the International Urban Design Course.

Alessandro Frigerio
PhD architect, urban and landscape designer, he works on urban regeneration processes and sustainable development with a focus on public space and landscape on a variety of scales and from an interdisciplinary perspective. He has dedicated himself to projects, consultancy, and research on these topics in Europe, Africa, and the Middle East, for various private developers, public institutions, and international cooperation agencies, including through his collaborations with the Politecnico di Milano, where he is involved in research and teaching activities. He is an associate of the AG&P greenscape studio, with which he has been collaborating for several years.

Gioia Gibelli
Architect, a graduate from the Politecnico di Milano in 1978 with a thesis on farmsteads and rural landscapes in the south-east of Milan. She works with landscape planning and design, with a focus on Landscape Ecology and on public and private landscape as a common good. She has won competitions and awards, some of them international, for the numerous plans and projects realised over the years. Councillor of the Parco Lombardo della Valle del Ticino from 2015 to 2019. Member of the FAI Board of Directors. Awarded the 'Earth Prize 2019 Italy' for Landscape. Author of 130 publications on landscape.

Simona Galateo
PhD architect, curator, and editor, she has written articles for magazines, including *Abitare*, *Domus*, *Arquitectura Viva*, *Artribune* and *Il Manifesto*, and edited books published with national and international publishers. She has curated numerous exhibitions on the main themes of contemporary architecture and has exhibited at the Italian Pavilion of the 12th Venice Architecture Biennale and at the Milan Triennale. In recent years she has carried out research on the themes of urban regeneration, and on the relationship between architecture, pedagogy, and landscape. She is currently involved in research at the Libera Università di Bolzano.

Acknowledgements

This book would not have been possible without the passionate commitment of the many people who have over the years worked and still work for AG&P greenscape.

We would also like to thank the important professionals who have shared their valuable thoughts in the book: Gioia Gibelli, Paolo Micheli, Francesco De Chio, Luigi Priano, Paolo Micucci, Roberto Russo, Stefano Boeri, the Crédit Agricole Italia team, Mattia Palazzi, and Francesca Colombo.

The support of many travel companions with whom we have undertaken fruitful collaborations that go beyond our work commitment has been fundamental in these years. Among them, we would particularly like to mention Giacomo Cocozza and his studio, the Arassociati studio, the RPBW studio, the MAB Arquitectura studio, Real Step, Marco Nolli, the Gucci group, the municipality of Mantua, the municipality of Savona, the municipality of Segrate, the municipality of Milano, the Zacchera Hotels group, the entire BAM - Fondazione Riccardo Catella team, and Tiziana Pollio for her invaluable support.

Lastly, we would like to thank all the people not explicitly mentioned who have collaborated with AG&P greenscape in the most diverse forms over the years, making this path of growth exciting in both professional and human terms.

Credits

All graphic designs for the book, except where otherwise indicated, were created and edited by the AG&P greenscape team with the special contribution of Igino Marchesin and Giulia Gigantino.

Photos
In alphabetical order

© Archivio Fotografico BAM - Photo by Elisabetta Brian: p. 255
© Archivio Fotografico BAM - Photo by Andrea Cherchi: p. 252
© Archivio Fotografico BAM - Photo by Dimitar Harizanov: p. 249
Chiara Battini: p. 105
Andrea Bortolotti: pp. 49, 50, 82, 117, 146, 239
Emanuele Bortolotti: p. 172
Alberto Callari: pp. 61, 66, 68, 117, 242, 243
Courtesy of Comitato Ponti: p. 81
Valerio Cozzi: p. 81
Matteo Cupella, 2021 © FAI: p. 201
© Antonio De Luca: cover, pp. 8, 14, 20, 28, 36
Ludovica De Ruvo: p. 254
Aurora Di Girolamo: p. 82
Sofya Dolgaya: p. 172
© Alberto Fanelli: p. 134
Barbara Frangi: pp. 117, 118, 236, 249
Alessandro Frigerio: pp. 90, 205
Dario Fusaro: p. 202
Irene Grieco: p. 206
© Indievolpe - Elisa Fumagalli: p. 146
Panovisioni by Franco Lanfredi: p. 198
Courtesy of Real Step - Photo by Carola Merello: p. 81
Aldo Rossi: p. 201
Courtesy of RPBW - Photo by Andrea Botto: pp. 99, 105
© Martina Santimone: pp. 104, 105, 217, 220, 226, 271
© Pietro Savorelli: pp. 46, 54, 61, 66, 70, 86, 130, 145, 148, 149, 168, 174, 175, 178, 184, 185, 187, 188, 210, 215, 217, 218, 222, 223, 224, 228, 270
Pierpaolo Tagliola: pp. 145, 171
Mariagiusi Troisi: pp. 118, 183, 200, 241, 246, 250, 254, 255

Renderings, drawings and graphics works
In alphabetical order

Massimo Brignoli: pp. 99, 122, 123, 207
Courtesy of Generali e BIG Bjarke Ingels Group - © B&TB: pp. 114, 133
Courtesy of Level Creative Studio: pp. 142, 160
© MAB arquitectura: p. 50
Paolo Maneo and Teresa di Muccio: pp. 52, 62, 84
Manica Architecture and Sportium: pp. 122, 123
© RPBW: pp. 88, 94
© RPBW-OBR: pp. 78, 100
RPBW-OBR: pp. 103, 106
Courtesy of Stefano Boeri Architetti: pp. 150, 157
Courtesy of Generali and BIG Bjarke Ingels Group - © Strutturaleggera: p. 133
Mariagiusi Troisi: p. 278
Courtesy of WOLF Visualization Agency: p. 82

Paolo Villa

Free and happy plants: an alternative

We are people of humble origins, with some ambitions in gardening, and perhaps this has confused us. We see fruit trees pruned to increase their production, hedges kept in shape, creepers reduced to contain their vitality. These types of plants need to be carefully tended every year to ensure a good harvest or an aesthetic result. Sometimes pruning is done for the safety of people and property, rarely for the survival of the plant and its well-being. Out of habit, we end up practising these actions on all plants. We impose geometric shapes, perfect forms on a nature we say we are inspired by, but in fact we prevent its free expression. The massacre of pruning not only demeans the trees, but also prevents them from teaching us the true nature they carry within.

I often stop to admire a plant, to photograph it, to draw it. Looking at the pictures again, I realise that they insistently portray the same subjects. They are generally broad-leaved trees that grow spontaneously and without anyone touching them. I always knew I had a soft spot for these plants, but I had never put them in the centre of attention: it was as if they remained a bit out of focus, at the edge of the frame. Comparing them with the rigid methods of nursery cultivation and planting in gardens and parks seeds some doubt in my mind about our supposed love of Nature. I fear that there has been a blackout with regard to our roots that has made us lose our familiarity with plants and the sense for which we do certain things. Traditions are one thing; mechanical and mindless actions are another.

Many trees have no cause to be pruned; they are wrong trees. They should have been chosen with due regard to the available space and then left to grow. A large shrub should be preferred to a tree, which will sooner or later oblige us to pick up the shears, leaving irreparable marks. They are not only ugly and affect growth but are the gateway to fungi and disease.

In every garden, park, green area, let us try to plant a plant, at least one, that can grow without being touched, without pruning, without being conditioned by our sense of aesthetics that responds to a limited way of seeing, devoid of imagination, love and pity.

Planting a beautiful plant does not mean digging a chasm, putting in a 300-year-old olive tree massacred by a carpenter disguised as a gardener and then boasting about the masterpiece. It means planting or letting grow a small plant, even a spontaneous one, something real, that contains only Nature and can teach us to read day by day, year by year, its joy of growing. More than teaching plants how they should grow, we must listen to what they have to tell us.

I have planted thousands of trees.
I have dreamed that all of them are happy.

The trees in the AG&P forest are a fascinating harmony of roots, trunks, branches, leaves, and flowers.
Some solitary, some companionable, all mature in parallel.

You can take in the scents, sounds, and atmospheres of the Bosco as soon as you enter.

Some leave space, some fill in the gaps, some conquer the air of heaven, and some leave abundant seeds.

The Bosco is grateful to generous plants.

Paolo Villa

Facing page:
the miniature forest made by Paolo Villa with azalea branches.

Paolo Villa (1958 - 2019)
Paolo Villa was one of the leading contemporary Italian landscape architects, capable of contributing with great passion to the debate on this discipline in our country. In 1985, with Emanuele Bortolotti, he founded the AG&P studio, with which he carried out his professional activity for more than thirty years in Italy and abroad. We at AG&P greenscape remember him as a mentor and a person of incredible human and professional qualities, still able to inspire us in our work today.

The Right to Nature

Published by
Actar Publishers, New York, Barcelona
www.actar.com

Authors
Emanuele Bortolotti, Paolo Palmulli
with Alessandro Frigerio

Edited by
Simona Galateo

Editorial coordination
Andrea Bortolotti

Graphic design
AG&P greenscape

Cover and illustrations design
Ginette Caron Communication Design
Ginette Caron and Masami Moriyama

Copy editing and proofreading
Greta Leoni and Valeria Carnevali

Printing and binding
Arlequin SL

Distribution
Actar D, Inc. New York, Barcelona

New York
440 Park Avenue South, 17th Floor
New York, NY 10016, USA
T +1 2129662207
salesnewyork@actar-d.com

Barcelona
Roca i Batlle 2
08023 Barcelona, Spain
T +34 933 282 183
eurosales@actar-d.com

Indexing
English ISBN: 978-1-63840-043-1
Library of Congress Control Number:
2022942866

Printed in Barcelona, Spain
Publication date: June 2024
Cover image: ©Antonio De Luca